SECRET LOUISVILLE

A GUIDE TO THE WEIRD, WONDERFUL, AND OBSCURE

Kevin Gibson

Copyright © 2017, Reedy Press, LLC
All rights reserved.
Reedy Press
PO Box 5131
St. Louis, MO 63139
www.reedypress.com

Library of Congress Control Number: 2016955976

ISBN: 9781681060712

Design by Jill Halpin

Printed in the United States of America
17 18 19 20 21 5 4 3 2 1

CONTENTS

INTRODUCTION

Louisville is indeed my city, but I don't know everything there is to know about her; boy, did that point ever come home to roost as I was writing this book. What awaits you are eighty-nine stories about interesting, fun, or just puzzling places, people, things, and historical facts that you might not know about—or if you do know about them, you might not know the full story. That's exactly what *Secret Louisville: A Guide to the Weird, Wonderful, and Obscure* is all about: I want to give you a view of Louisville you may never have seen before.

In writing this book, I found myself driving all over the metro area, to the far reaches of Louisville's outskirts and across the river into Indiana, looking for all things weird and wonderful. I found myself moved by a prayer grotto and spooked by a hidden cave. My heart was touched by an out-of-the-way animal farm, and I marveled at an island getaway on the Ohio River that is easily accessible by a small bridge. It was quite a journey.

But again, the highlight of the journey for me is that I learned even more about my city than I had already known from living in it and covering it as a food and beverage writer, not to mention the years I spent covering news, arts, and sports. What I hope is that I can share some of that experience with you, the reader, and possibly inspire you to get into your car or onto your bike and explore the unique spaces and experiences I've laid out in the pages that follow.

Hey, there's only so much you can learn on social media—so, let's go discover Louisville together.

ACKNOWLEDGMENTS

I owe so much to my wonderful friends and acquaintances for the successful completion of this book. I had a blast compiling the ideas and seeking out the different stories and locations, but I also got a boost simply by asking people what they would include in the list of fun and weird Louisville spots and histories if they were writing a book. My people responded, and responded well.

And so, I will send out some thank-yous, starting with my lovely and patient girlfriend Cynthia Bard, who is unwavering in her support of me and my hours and hours spent writing all the things that I write. Cynthia is an amazing friend and support system. Her wonderful son Nikolai is equally patient when he gets dragged along to investigate, and his smile is a bright light in times when there is darkness. I also must thank my supportive parents, Ron and Jula Gibson, as well as my faithful dog Darby, who seems to just go with whatever flow I bring home. My son Scott, his fiancée Kayla, and my soon-to-be granddaughter Jaelynn are also in my circle of love. And then there are my close friends like Butch and Jane Bays, Greg and Jeanette Thomas, and Jerry and Cindy Mason. Gosh, there are so many more—I truly have the best circle of friends and family on earth. (I wish I could name them all, but this book is only 186 pages long.)

And there are a few folks I must thank who helped provide ideas, inspiration, assistance, and/or photos for this book (in no particular order): David Wicks, Tracy Karem, Terry Meiners, Ken Hardin, Robin Garr, Leigh Ann Yost, Fred Minnick, Michael Moeller, Andrea Blair, C.J. Cumberland, Dylan Greenwood, Kim Mays, Jeanette Thomas, Maggie Kimberl, Hill Harcourt, Moe Loughran, Eerie Indiana, Bob Cole, Andrew Johnson, Elizabeth Reilly, Katie Munich, Ben Schneider, Nathan Salsburg, Kevin Ratterman, Mike Ratterman, Andy Harpole, Jeremy Priddy, Melissa Amos Jones, and everyone I've forgotten. Thank you!

1 THE CHICKENS CAME HOME TO ROOST

What is this hidden and mysterious set of stairs?

Marked only by an easily-missed sign along lower Brownsboro Road, the Chicken Steps offer a means for travelers on foot to either ascend to Vernon Avenue, connecting them with busy Frankfort Avenue, or to descend in the opposite direction. The spot on Vernon where the steps begin their descent is the one-time location of Fort Elstner, one of eleven Union forts constructed to defend Louisville during the Civil War. (In fact, an artillery gun was mounted on the spot that is now 188 Vernon Avenue.)

The thing is, no one is one hundred percent sure why they're called "the Chicken Steps"—that's just what they've always been called. Some believe the steps, which number thirty-five including the midway landing, may have gotten their name because chickens used to roost on an earlier wooden version. (The current concrete ones were constructed by the city in the 1970s.)

A 2003 report from Louisville Metro Planning and Design Services notes, "The name 'Chicken Steps' likely came about from the days when area residents raised chickens, some of which chose this hilltop site upon which to roost."

Hey, regardless of where the name originates, it beats climbing down that hill.

Coming down the hill, the pathway leads you right past CVS. Might as well grab some allergy medicine while you're there.

CHICKEN STEPS

WHAT A hidden set of stairs

WHERE Tucked in a wooded area between Vernon Ave. and lower Brownsboro Rd.

COST Free

PRO TIP The Chicken Steps offer safe passage to Lower Brownsboro for the visually-impaired who live in the neighborhood near the Printing House for the Blind.

The Chicken Steps feature thirty-five steps, including the landing midway. Photo by the author.

2 NOW THAT'S A BIG CLOCK

What is that gigantic illuminated clock overlooking the river?

With a diameter of forty feet, the Colgate Clock was first illuminated in Clarksville, Indiana, on November 17, 1924. The clock face is actually larger than those on the legendary Big Ben, which is located at the Palace of Westminster in London, and is to this day one of the largest clocks in the world. It was installed shortly after Colgate-Palmolive converted a pre-Civil War correctional facility—which still housed prisoners who even helped with the conversion while incarcerated—into a soap-making plant.

An enduring vision in downtown Louisville for as long as locals can remember, the bright red clock (when lit) usually shows the correct time, or at least close, nearly one hundred years later, despite the fact that Colgate-Palmolive moved its operations out of town in 2008. The clock's continuing operation is likely because the facility was placed on the Indiana Landmarks list of 10 Most Endangered landmarks, although the clock's life is not necessarily guaranteed. Interestingly, the Colgate clock originally was designed and built in 1906, and was located in Jersey City, New Jersey, at

---

If you're in Clarksville without your watch or phone and need to see what time it is, you'll potentially have to drive across the Clark Bridge to use the Colgate Clock for time-telling.

COLGATE CLOCK

WHAT Gigantic illuminated clock

WHERE Clarksville, IN

COST General admission is $12

PRO TIP One of the largest clocks on the planet, you can still enjoy it illuminated in red most nights.

The Colgate Clock has been keeping time on the Ohio River since 1924. Photo by the author.

Colgate's original factory before being moved to the newly-opened factory in Indiana in '24.

Of course, the joke among locals is that the clock is located in one state but can only be read in another. "Leave it to Indiana to put up a clock you have to drive to Kentucky to read," my uncle once joked. Ah well, at least the view is nice.

3 IT MUST BE A SIGN

Why is there a donut sign . . . on a pizza joint?

The St. Matthews area of Louisville, a junction packed with restaurants and storefronts from an Irish pub to a German bakery, keeps things bustling and active. And right smack in the middle of it is a huge, cartoonish sign featuring a googly-eyed baker and the words, "Baker Boy Inc. Hot Donuts." (The "o" in the word "donuts" is, of course, a cartoon donut.)

The sign was uncovered during renovations by Mellow Mushroom, which in 2012 took over a space that, in part, once housed a local dive bar known as Dutch's Tavern. But when Mellow Mushroom began tearing the façade off the building to remodel the space, they found the sign peeking from behind the rubble. Known for its kitschy décor anyway, the restaurant group decided to leave the sign right where it was. But oddly, no one in Louisville could remember a business called Baker Boy Hot Donuts, or any donut shop ever being in the location.

However, a local Realtor named Brad Long set out to solve the mystery, and finally did—sort of. Apparently, there had been a soda shop near that location during Prohibition, and once 1933 rolled around, that shop was quickly converted into a tavern. That probably was the forebear of Dutch's. But

---

There is a company named Baker Boy based out west, but it isn't related to the Louisville sign.

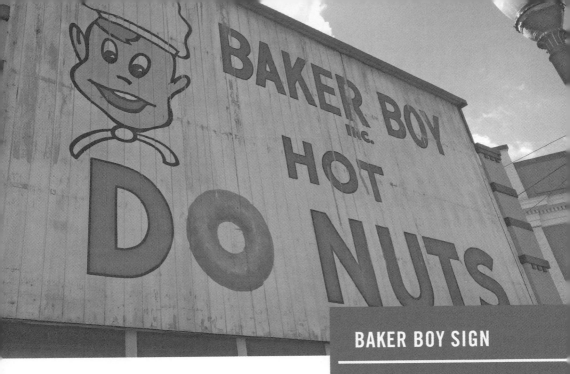

The Baker Boy Donuts sign was uncovered in 2012. Photo by the author.

where do the donuts come in? Best guess is that it was a brand of donuts sold at the soda shop during that time. But wait . . . the sign sure looks like 1940s- or '50s-era vintage. So, who knows where the truth lies?

BAKER BOY SIGN

WHAT An old advertising sign

WHERE 3920 Shelbyville Rd.

COST Free (unless you order pizza)

PRO TIP No one seems completely sure why it's there, so if you can solve the mystery once and for all, please share.

4 LOUISVILLE, HOME OF THE CHEESEBURGER . . . MAYBE

Is the meat sandwich with cheese truly a Louisville original?

Per local legend, sometime during 1934 Carl Kaelin had the grand idea to plop a slice of American cheese onto a hamburger patty. His restaurant was called Kaelin's, the new spin on a simple burger was a hit, and a lasting cultural phenomenon was the result. Ask most any Louisvillian about the history of the cheeseburger, and they'll mention Kaelin's. Before the restaurant closed in 2004 (the building is still there and looks pretty much as it always did), it still bore a sign claiming itself as the birthplace of the culinary wonder.

But is that claim valid? Depends on who you ask. In 1935, for instance, Louis Ballast of the Humpty Dumpty Drive-In in Denver filed a trademark claim on the word "cheeseburger." But people were putting cheese on hamburgers before all that. In fact, most non-Louisvillians credit Lionel Sternberger for the invention in 1924. According to About.com, Sternberger, age sixteen, "decided to slap a slice of American cheese (what else?) on to a cooking hamburger at

---

Word is the new owner of the Kaelin's property is working on a new restaurant concept for the spot.

Kaelin's is now closed, but many believe it to be the birthplace of the cheese-burger. Public domain photo/Wikimedia Commons.

his father's Pasadena, California, sandwich shop, the Rite Spot."

But the Rite Spot apparently called it a "cheese hamburger." So, technically, the name "cheeseburger" may not have been coined until Kaelin's decided to add cheese, even if the local restaurant wasn't technically the first one to the punch. So, if someone in Louisville tells you the cheeseburger was invented here, tell them you have a secret you'd like to share about the cheese hamburger.

KAELIN'S RESTAURANT

WHAT A local restaurant legend

WHERE Kaelin's Restaurant (now closed)

COST Free

PRO TIP It's been long debated, but Louisville still claims the cheeseburger.

THE LAST DRIVE-IN PICTURE SHOW

Why did all the drive-in theaters die? Well . . .

We've been watching the American drive-in movie theater slowly die off. In the heyday of the drive-in movie craze, there were more than four thousand such theaters operating in the U.S., according to *USA Today*. As recently as 1980, there were about twenty-four hundred still around. But many factors slowly but surely took their toll, from cable TV to the rise of digital filmography and projection, and today there are fewer than 350 still in business. In Louisville, the drive-in theater is no more, the last breath ceasing with the closing of the Kenwood Drive-In back in 2009. It is truly extinct.

But wait . . . there is another.

Across the Ohio River and about fifteen miles east is a tiny town called Georgetown, Indiana. Originally opened in 1951 as a single-screen drive-in, the drive-in there now boasts two screens, not to mention the original snack bar in the center of the uneven grassy field with murals of a hamburger and a hot

The Georgetown Drive-In hasn't changed much over the last forty-five-plus years. Photos by the author.

dog on its side, the original "box office" window at the gate, and even upgraded FM stereo sound.

The Georgetown Drive-In is so steeped in Americana that there is a turquoise 1957 Chevy, decked out with neon to help guide visitors to the entrance through dark Indiana nights, on top of the two-faced vintage sign trumpeting what's playing. Heck, there's even an attached fireworks store—it doesn't get much more American than that.

GEORGETOWN DRIVE-IN

WHAT A surviving drive-in theater

WHERE 8200 S.R. 64, Georgetown, IN

COST $6-$11 (cash only)

PRO TIP If you go, get there early—the Georgetown Drive-In is known to fill up, especially if the movies being shown are new and popular. And be prepared for a line of cars down the street on S.R. 64.

Georgetown Drive-In is one of the few American drive-in theaters remaining that still has a playground.

<u>6</u> THE HIDDEN MUSIC HALL

What's behind the blue door set into that stone hillside façade?

Behind a blue door set into a hillside lies an underground cavern, rumored to have once been used to lager and store beer. But these days, the Workhouse Ballroom is a narrow stone structure hidden away from the elements and used for hosting events like concerts and receptions. Some call it simply, "The Cave." A local publication, *The Paper*, referred to it as "The Cave of Underground Sounds."

But there's mystery in its history, thanks to decade upon decade of speculation. Owner Mike Ratterman told *The Paper* he had found newspaper articles from the 1850s identifying the space as a beer lagering cellar, but there are other myths about the place as well.

Whatever formerly went on beneath that hill, we know what happens now, and it's a well-kept secret: music. It's sort of like Louisville's version of Liverpool, England's, The Cavern Club, where the Beatles rose to prominence in the early 1960s. Perhaps a similar legend will rise from this local cavern.

THE CAVE OF UNDERGROUND SOUNDS

WHAT A cavern turned music venue

WHERE 1312 Lexington Rd.

COST Varies

PRO TIP No is one hundred percent certain why the cave exists in the first place, but it's sure worth catching a show.

A former beer cellar is now a concert hall. Photo Above, courtesy of Mike Ratterman. Left, photo by the author.

One theory about the cavern is that it was once used as a debtor's prison, with its identifying shackles and bars being removed for scrap metal years ago.

THE TROLL IN THE ALLEY

Why is there a freaky-looking creature stalking a downtown alley?

While hip locals know where the Troll Pub Under the Bridge is located, it isn't something you're likely to just stumble across by accident. Situated on the original location of the world-famous Galt House hotel, built in 1834, the Troll Pub is now part of an 1877 structure that once was the Louisville and Nashville Railroad's headquarters.

The 1937 Flood, however, put not only much of the building but all of West Washington Street under water. The space where the Troll Pub exists now was later filled in with dirt and debris after spending time in the 1970s as an artist colony. However, in 2010, a developer saw opportunity: The space was cleaned out and restored as a cozy pub and restaurant which sits in the shadow of the Clark Memorial Bridge just a few steps from the Yum! Center, a twenty-two-thousand-capacity, multi-use venue. The Troll Pub is always packed with customers any time there is an event.

The troll statue welcomes all who walk by into the underground pub, and a sign further invites everyone to stop for a photo. It's a selfie-stick owner's dream.

The troll's name is Louie.

The troll is a popular photo-op spot in downtown Louisville. Photo by the author.

TROLL PUB

WHAT A giant troll statue

WHERE 150 W Washington St.

COST Free (unless you stop in for a drink or a snack)

PRO TIP The troll is a top Louisville photo opportunity for tourists and natives alike, so be sure to snap a selfie.

SHOES DON'T GROW ON TREES . . . OR DO THEY?

Is this mysterious tree sprouting shoes?

Down a lonely country road, in a random spot a few miles south of tiny Milltown, Indiana—known mostly for its Blue River canoe attractions—is a curiosity and tourist attraction that once drew thousands of people from around the world. It is known only as the Milltown Shoe Tree.

At some point many decades ago—perhaps the early 1970s, as one blogger guessed—people began tossing their shoes over the branches of a tree not far from where Pilot Knob Road intersects Devil's Hollow Road. Tennis shoes, basketball shoes, street shoes, even flip-flops can be found in the tree.

Thing is, no one is totally sure who started it, or why. One local woman told a news reporter several years ago that her cousin and a few friends were wading through a nearby creek, got their shoes wet, and for fun, decided to simply toss them up into the tree, tied together by the laces.

That assertion remains unconfirmed. Nor is anyone sure why people kept on throwing more shoes into the tree, or even how word spread about the tree, making it a tourist attraction. It is simply a local legend. (Another legend has it that NBA Hall of Famer Larry Bird, an Indiana native, once tossed a pair of his size thirteen sneakers into the tree. This is also unconfirmed.)

MILLTOWN SHOE TREE

WHAT A mysterious tree covered with shoes

WHERE Milltown, IN

COST Free

PRO TIP Keep your eyes peeled for a little place along the road where a car could turn around—that's where the tree is located.

*The current shoe tree has fewer shoes
than its predecessor, but it's growing.
Photo by the author.*

*The original shoe tree, before it was
struck by lightning. Photo courtesy of
Eerie Indiana.*

However, some years ago, the original tree was struck by
lightning and badly damaged. The legend of the shoe tree
seemed to be over, and there was apparently even discussion
of cutting the tree down. But a good legend perseveres. People
have continued visiting the spot and tossing shoes into the
remaining tree and nearby trees. They're tough to see if you
aren't paying attention—I drove right by it while hunting for it
during my research for this book—but it's worth a stop, even if it
is quite a haul west on Interstate 64.

No one seems to throw their socks into
the tree, but you could be the first.

9 THE SECRET GARDEN

What does that suburban path lead to?

The Belknap area is a quiet, well-kept suburban neighborhood adjacent to the popular Highlands. But like so many neighborhoods, Belknap has a secret. Well, a secret garden at least, so well hidden between two houses that it would be easy to walk right past—assuming one didn't notice the bear statue welcoming visitors.

From the entrance, you walk down a wooded path, past a memorial garden with a bench, and into a clearing complete with a gazebo, a bridge, locally-created artwork that is literally carved right into the trees, and even climbing and playground equipment, not to mention a few nice spots for a picnic lunch. That's Warheim Park.

Originally an overgrown area that was for years used as a dumping ground, the lot was purchased by Hal Warheim in 1974. He knew it had potential, so he set out to clean out the grounds and make it available to the public, doing so over the course of several years.

WARHEIM PARK

WHAT A hidden park

WHERE 1832 Overlook Terr.

COST Free

PRO TIP The entrance to the park is situated between a couple of houses. Just look for the wooden sign and the friendly bear.

"I dragged a stove, a sofa, bags of beer cans out of here," Warheim told me. "All kinds of junk."

Some thirty years later, the dream was realized, and what is now called Warheim Park was born. Neighborhood resident Katie Gaughan says it never gets old watching children react when they finally see the welcoming statue by the park's entrance.

Warheim Park is like an oasis in a residential neighborhood near the Highlands. Photos by the author.

"They start yelling, 'Guys, I found it, I found it! I found the secret park!'" she said.

Now, you can find it too.

Kids often call it "Frog Park," because it is inhabited by a friendly green frog statue in the park's center.

10 LOUISVILLE WAS A KEY PART OF THE UNDERGROUND RAILROAD

Did you know that secret tunnels beneath a local church helped guide slaves to freedom?

Now known as the Second Baptist Church, the former Town Clock Church in New Albany, Indiana, built in 1857 just across the Ohio River from Louisville, has been called "the gateway to the Underground Railroad," the network that helped slaves find freedom leading up to and during the Civil War. There are a series of tunnels beneath the church that were used as hideouts and as secret passageways to other destinations.

Of course, Louisville's location on the Ohio River made it a hub for slave trading. In fact, there were several "slave pens" in Louisville's downtown, one of them at the intersection of Main and Second Streets, now a busy thoroughfare connecting downtown to Indiana by way of the Clark Memorial Bridge. Slave auctions were held downtown on a regular basis, with slave traders often bringing them in by boat.

But the proximity of Louisville to a "free" state also made

The term "sold down the river" is believed to have originated in Louisville as part of a slave trade that would send slaves down the Ohio River to New Orleans.

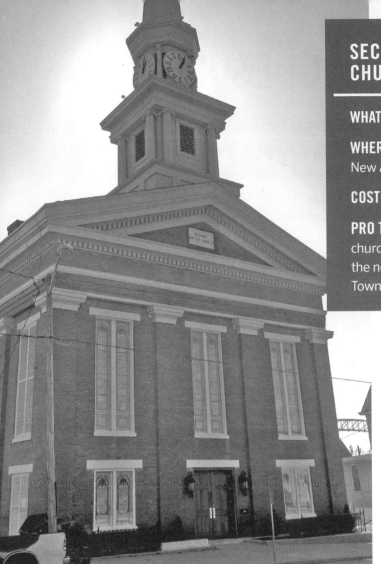

SECOND BAPTIST CHURCH

WHAT A historic church

WHERE 300 E Main St., New Albany, IN

COST Free

PRO TIP You can help the old church survive by donating to the non-profit Friends of the Town Clock Church.

The Second Baptist Church, formerly the Town Clock Church, lives on as a symbol of freedom. Photo by the author.

it a place where slaves could find passage out of the South and into freedom, assuming they could escape from their owners and not be chased down and extradited. Some would sneak onto ferries, while others would swim across, float across on makeshift rafts, walk across on sandbars, or even make their way across during winter months when the river would occasionally freeze over. Many made it to the Town Clock Church and found new lives, and the church still stands in New Albany as a symbol of freedom that is being restored and is part of New Albany's Downtown Historic District. It recently received a new steeple and is undergoing restoration.

11 ELEVEN JONES CAVE

Was this small cave once the hideout of bank robbers?

Once upon a time, as legend has it, a family of eleven brothers with the surname Jones used a small cave situated in Beargrass Creek, a few miles inland from the Ohio River, as a hideout. The ne'er-do-well brothers were bank robbers, counterfeiters, and murderers, and they stashed their loot inside the cave.

According to this legend, the Jones boys also created separate rooms deep inside the cavern, and multiple entrances were said to exist. Other stories about the cave give rise to it having been much larger, and some believed the Jones treasure was still buried deep inside. Some stories even say the cave, which was first known as Eleven Jones Cave in 1848, was guarded by a cannon. There allegedly is also a metal gate that is believed to have helped keep others from stealing the Jones loot, and other tales suggest supernatural goings-on.

But the truth is the cave entrance isn't large enough for a full-grown man to walk into at just four feet high and two feet wide. Sure, my father tells me stories of his friends and him going into the cave as kids, but buried treasure?

Eleven Jones Cave is the only known habitat for Louisville cave beetles, a species that is currently identified as a candidate for endangered species status.

ELEVEN JONES CAVE

WHAT A legendary cave

WHERE Beargrass Creek, near Poplar Level Rd.

COST Free

PRO TIP The cave is located along Beargrass Creek near Louisville Cemetery.

Eleven Jones Cave isn't even big enough for someone to walk into these days. Photo by Bedford/Public Domain/Wikimedia.

These days, reports say the air inside the cave is not suitable for breathing, so there's little chance we'll ever know for sure what lies inside. Well, other than a natural spring and a lot of beetles.

12 THE CRASHED AIRPLANE ON THE HILL

Why didn't anyone clean up the wreckage of a plane that flew into the side of a hill?

Back in the 1980s, a lone pilot in a single engine aircraft flying over Louisville found himself unable to make it back to Standiford Field airport due to engine trouble. The red and white plane went down, crashing into a hillside near Distillery Commons, a former distilling operation turned commerce center. Miraculously, the pilot was uninjured, and his plane was left behind as part of the landscaping.

Wait—that's just the legendary story that has been told or at least speculated upon since the late 1980s, yet not everyone these days knows the real story. The plane was actually placed there by the owner of a bar named Cliffhangers that was located above Distillery Commons. It was a prop, something to draw attention, and originally there was even a parachute with a mannequin hanging from the wreckage. But after the bar closed, the plane stayed.

The concert venue next to the plane, Headliners Music Hall, draws an audience of young customers who, no doubt, notice the plane and wonder what gives.

PLANE LANDSCAPE

WHAT A downed airplane

WHERE 1386 Lexington Rd.

COST Free

PRO TIP If you look closely, you can see the supports that keep the small plane suspended along the hillside.

The old airplane model is slowly being swallowed up by the trees.
Photo by the author.

And stayed, and stayed. Nearly thirty years later, tattered and covered in graffiti, the plane still pokes from the trees that have grown up around it. In another twenty years, it will likely be completely overtaken.

But in the meantime, people continue to ask the question of how the plane got there. The legend lives on as a result.

13 LOUISVILLE, DISCO (BALL) CITY

Where do all the disco balls come from, anyway?

Located in a nondescript building in the Irish Hill neighborhood, Omega National Products doesn't seem like it would be anything more notable than just another Louisville business. But Omega National Products has a secret: it's the place where many, if not most, of the world's disco balls are produced. That's right: Louisville is Disco City.

You even have to dig into the company's website a bit to find their selection of "mirror balls" (very clever, Omega National). When you finally find the list, you can see that disco balls up to forty-eight inches in diameter and weighing 105 pounds are available; you may prefer a twenty-pounder, or perhaps the wee MG-12 model, which is a foot in diameter and a mere five pounds. Otherwise, check out Omega's selection of antique-style mirrors, which is impressive in its own right.

Then it's time to put on your platform shoes and do your thing.

A group called "World's Largest Disco Ball, Ya'll" hopes to create the largest disco ball in the world and gift it to Louisville, honoring the city's status as disco ball capital of the world.

It's like the 1970s never left us. Photo by Omega National Products.

OMEGA NATIONAL PRODUCTS

WHAT A disco ball factory

WHERE 900 Baxter Ave.

COST Depends on the size of the ball you want

PRO TIP Sorry, they don't have a dance floor at Omega National Products.

14 REMNANTS OF ROSE ISLAND

Why is there an old swimming pool in the middle of the woods?

Once upon a time, Rose Island entertained locals and travelers alike from its spot along the Ohio River across from Prospect, Kentucky. Opened in 1923, there was a hotel, a swimming pool, a Ferris wheel, a wooden roller coaster, and pony rides. There were even guest cottages for folks wanting to stay a couple of days, and often Louisvillians would travel to the park by ferry for a day of sun and fun.

Unfortunately, the 1937 Flood that submerged much of Louisville had other plans for the popular park. The flood crested at eighty-five-plus feet just downstream near downtown Louisville—that was a full thirty feet over flood level. In other words, Rose Island was almost completely washed away. The park's ownership never rebuilt the popular destination, and the skeleton of the park has been rotting away ever since, becoming part of the forest.

However, since the state park opened a few years ago, a replica of the original Rose Island sign has been placed

Rose Island is situated on a peninsula known as "Devil's Backbone."

The Rose Island swimming pool back in the day, and a shot of what is left today. Photos courtesy of Eerie Indiana.

to mark the spot, complete with photos and history of the park. It's not necessarily an easy hike to find the ruins, but it's worth the effort to see such a historical site that has been forgotten by many.

ROSE ISLAND

WHAT An abandoned old park

WHERE Charlestown State Park, 12500 Indiana 62

COST $7 park admission

PRO TIP Take hiking trail 3 to trail 7 to find Rose Island. If you make it to the bridge over 12-Mile Creek, you're almost there.

15 THE HISTORIC LOUISVILLE PUMPING STATION

You mean the Water Tower is more than just an event space?

These days, most Louisvillians know the Water Tower as a beautiful old venue for concerts, art exhibits, and the like, complete with a huge lawn for parking, stages, and more. But when the structure was conceived and built in the 1860s, it was done so out of fear for public safety. Prior to the pumping station, which was at the time the largest in the world, Louisville was known as "the graveyard of the west" because so much of the population was dying from cholera and typhoid. The cause? Tainted water. (This is one reason why bourbon was so widely consumed in Kentucky.)

This discovery came in the early 1850s, but the "theory" of tainted water and the proposal to build a pumping station were met with indifference, if not resistance. But when the station, designed by Theodore Scowden with its signature tower, statues, and Classical Revival architectural design, was finally finished, it was not only beautiful, it also could pump twelve million gallons of water out of the Ohio River every twenty-four hours. And the happy result was that by the early 1870s, cholera was gone from Louisville.

On the back side of the station, facing the Ohio River, is a marker showing where the 1937 Flood crested.

WATER TOWER

WHAT A historic landmark on the Ohio River

WHERE 3005 River Rd.

COST $5 or less for a tour; free to gaze at when passing by

PRO TIP Next time you have a nice, clear glass of Louisville water, you can thank this structure.

This historic pumping station helped save a lot of lives. Photos by the author.

The Water Tower is now on the National Register of Historic Places and houses a WaterWorks Museum which tells the history and importance of the station. It is a history worth exploring.

16 A CEMETERY'S TORTURED SECRET

Isn't that cemetery part of Cave Hill?

Not long ago, Eastern Cemetery, tucked into a bustling Highlands neighborhood and surrounded by bars and restaurants, was not just in disrepair—it was the subject of a gruesome and tortured scandal. Dating to the 1840s, it was one of the first cemeteries in the city to bury people of varying ethnicities and religions, from slaves to Catholic priests.

Steeped in history, the building at the front of the property—which is now home to residential apartments—once was the first crematorium in Kentucky. In the center of the cemetery sits an ornamental structure that looks like an elaborate crypt but actually acted as a "wake house" where families could say goodbye to their deceased relatives. In those days, most wakes or funerals were held in private homes, but the fear of disease contracted from having a dead body in the house was on the rise. In essence, that building was the first—or at least one of the first—iterations of a funeral home in Louisville.

But years later, the cemetery became the center of a scandal when it was discovered that the owners had for years been burying bodies on top of bodies in mass graves; the practice apparently dated back as far as the 1920s or

A documentary titled Facing East, detailing the cemetery's sordid history, was released in early 2017 to help raise awareness.

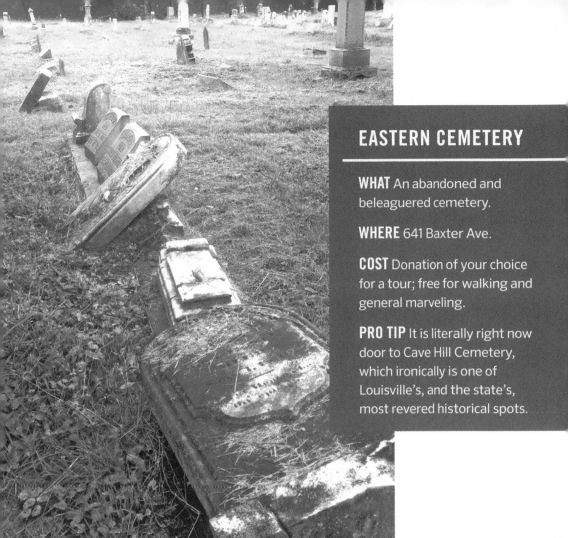

EASTERN CEMETERY

WHAT An abandoned and beleaguered cemetery.

WHERE 641 Baxter Ave.

COST Donation of your choice for a tour; free for walking and general marveling.

PRO TIP It is literally right now door to Cave Hill Cemetery, which ironically is one of Louisville's, and the state's, most revered historical spots.

The once-forgotten cemetery is finding new life thanks to local volunteers. Photo by the author.

even beyond. The cemetery came to national notoriety in the late 1980s when a worker reported the practice to Kentucky's State Attorney General.

Eastern Cemetery was left abandoned for decades, making it the victim of vandalism and general disrepair, but in recent years a group called Friends of Eastern Cemetery has been working to restore the cemetery, replace broken grave markers, and keep the grounds maintained. A recent documentary sheds new light on the cemetery, and fund-raising historical walking tours are helping to give the cemetery a brighter future.

THE MYSTERIOUS HISTORY OF THE BAXTER MORGUE

Sure, it's a fun attraction in the fall, but what was it before it was a haunted house?

Opened in 1901 just a few blocks from Louisville's largest cemetery, Cave Hill, Vanderdark Morgue (even the name is creepy) spent its first three decades as a thriving business not far from downtown Louisville. And then things got weird: on October 3, 1932, owner Victor Vanderdark disappeared. Gone. Poof.

Victor's son Warren took over the family business, but Warren's wife and young daughter also went missing without a trace two years later. In the meantime, business had begun to decline as reports of bizarre happenings began to leak out of the morgue. Warren changed the name to Baxter Avenue Morgue to deflect negative publicity, but the business couldn't be saved. Worse, weird happenings continued after the place went empty: weird smells, missing pets, missing people, and strange sounds were associated with the place, until finally, in 1951, it all stopped.

The building lay empty for years, until one day city inspectors were seen going into the building—and yet they declined to report what they'd found inside. When

---

Many of the personal artifacts from the Vanderdark family are now on display at the haunted house attraction.

BAXTER MORGUE

WHAT A former morgue

WHERE 451 Baxter Ave.

COST $20

PRO TIP The place is locked up most of the year, but worth the wait for Halloween season.

The entrance to Baxter Avenue Morgue. Photo by the author.

the space was finally purchased by private investors in the 1990s, it was only then that the history of the Vanderdark family was revealed, mostly by way of personal artifacts found in the basement. The space is now the subject of paranormal investigations as a severely haunted place.

Businesses operate in other parts of the building; the haunted house sits idle during off-seasons. Having walked through the haunted house portion personally, though, trust me: if they took away all the manufactured scares and decorations, it would be a much scarier place. It just has a creepy feel to it. You have been warned.

COBBLESTONE AND BRICK STREETS OF LOUISVILLE

What might lie beneath these streets that could date to the late 1700s?

Back when horses and carriages, along with trolleys, got people to and from wherever they were going, most of Louisville's roads were laid with cobblestone or brick. As concrete came to the fore, many of those roads were pulled up or simply covered over—in fact, much of downtown Louisville's roadways are concrete poured over cobblestone. And under those cobblestones is earth that has neither seen the light of day nor been touched by human hands since at least the 1800s. Who knows what might be buried beneath these roads?

One example of a cobblestone way is the alley that runs parallel to East Main Street, known as Billy Goat Strut Alley. It was originally cobblestone, but was paved over, and now pavement that has crumbled with age has revealed parts of the original street. One stretch of the alley just off Campbell is entirely exposed.

The historic Clifton neighborhood is peppered with cobblestone and

A view of Embry Avenue, looking towards Pope Street. Photo by the author.

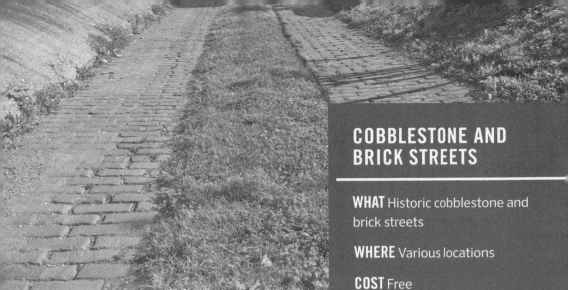

COBBLESTONE AND BRICK STREETS

WHAT Historic cobblestone and brick streets

WHERE Various locations

COST Free

PRO TIP If you ride over one of the streets on your bike or in your car, say, "Aaaah" the entire way. You'll feel like a kid again.

A view of Billy Goat Strut Alley. Photo by the author.

brick streets, including the entirety of the admittedly short Embry Avenue, situated between Pope and William Streets, as well as part of an alley that juts off west of the street. Talk about a little slice of history.

Not far from there is the slope at the end of several streets parallel to Pope, near Lower Brownsboro Road. Others include State Street between Frankfort and North Charlton Streets; Stevenson Avenue at Mellwood Avenue; the alley downtown behind Billy Goat Strut; portions of nearby Nanny Goat Strut, another alley; and the two blocks of South State Street.

In nearby Bardstown, Kentucky, you can find what is believed to be one of the oldest paved roads in all of Kentucky— it was laid around 1790 and was part of the legendary "Wilderness Road."

19 INFLUENCE OF THE SOUTHERN EXPOSITION

Why are there so many huge Victorian mansions in Old Louisville?

You probably know Louisville has one of the largest habitable Victorian neighborhoods in the U.S. Do you know why that is? Well, it is due in part to a land grant that dates back to 1772, when Louisville was being founded. But a development nearly one hundred years later kicked off construction of homes for and by the wealthy—that was the Southern Exposition.

The exposition intended to "advance the material welfare of the producing classes of the South and West," according to then *Courier-Journal* editor Henry Watterson. The five-year exposition included a series of one-hundred-day events similar to the World's Fair that highlighted advancements in technology, industry, agriculture, art, and more.

The Southern Exposition so buoyed Louisville's profile and potential for growth that the forty-five acres where it took place soon were home to development, including mansions and St. James Court. Developed then to be a haven for wealthy residents in the neighborhood, it is now the annual site of one of the country's most respected art festivals.

A postcard promoting the Southern Exposition. Public domain photo/Wikimedia Commons.

One of the selling points of the exposition was its ability to remain open at night, thanks to what then was the largest-ever display of incandescent light bulbs.

SOUTHERN EXPOSITION

WHAT A historic event that shaped Louisville

WHERE Immediately south of Central Park in the St. James area.

COST Free

PRO TIP Visit the Victorian Mansions in Old Louisville and you'll be in the heart of what was the Southern Exposition.

BASEBALL GREATS TO NEGRO LEAGUE ATHLETES PLAYED AT PARKWAY FIELD

Isn't that field just for intramural sports?

These days, Parkway Field is a small component of the University of Louisville campus, an athletic field that plays host to intramural soccer and football games. And while the grandstands and outfield walls of the original field have all been demolished, many sports legends once traversed the area that remains.

Parkway was the home of the minor-league Louisville Colonels from 1923 until 1956, and many future Hall of Famers played ball there. For instance, Jackie Robinson played his first-ever professional baseball game at Parkway Field in 1946, and the stadium was the home of several Negro League teams. Babe Ruth and Lou Gehrig did barnstorming dates at Parkway in 1928, as did Satchel Paige, all of whom are now in the Baseball Hall of Fame.

So, next time you are near Louisville's campus, stop

Other sports legends to play baseball or football on Parkway Field include Pee Wee Reese, Johnny Bench, Billy Herman, Earl Combs, and Johnny Unitas.

Presented With the Compliments of

LOUISVILLE BASEBALL CLUB, STATION WAVE

and the

OERTEL BREWING COMPANY

Who Bring You All Broadcasts of the Louisville Colonels' Baseball Games

RADIO APPRECIATION NIGHT AUGUST 5, 1947

DON HILL
Oertel Sports Reporter
WAVE

BRUCE DUDLEY
Louisville Baseball Club
PRESIDENT

A Louisville Colonels team photo presented to fans in the 1940s.
Photo courtesy of the author.

by and take a step or two onto the intramural field and soak up the magic; it's the site where many sports greats played decades ago in Louisville. Who knows, maybe you'll soak up enough of that long-ago magic to finally be able to hit a curveball.

PARKWAY FIELD

WHAT A former baseball field where legends once played

WHERE The intersection of Crittenden Dr. and S Brook St.

COST Free

PRO TIP The green bricks in the supports of the University of Louisville's current baseball stadium, Jim Patterson Stadium, are actually bricks from Parkway Field's outfield wall.

LOUISVILLE IS SO MONEY

How did ancient Roman coins manage to find their way to Louisville?

Louisville is well known for its Falls of the Ohio, home to one of the oldest known exposed fossil beds on planet Earth. And while ancient Rome doesn't date back nearly as far as the Devonian Period (some 380 million years ago), we know that the so-called "New World" wasn't set to be inhabited until many centuries after the fall of Rome.

Which is why a discovery made in 1963 as crews were beginning construction on the Sherman Minton Bridge, connecting New Albany, Indiana, with Louisville's west end, seems so strange. During excavation, a worker uncovered a handful of Roman coins, one of them depicting Emperor Claudius II.

The coins are believed to have originated somewhere between 238 and 305 A.D. They were on display for a time at the Falls of the Ohio State Park Interpretive Center but, per the book *Weird Kentucky*, the state of Indiana apparently has a strict policy on anything suggesting that explorers found the New World before Christopher Columbus.

But it wasn't the only such

ROMAN COINS

WHAT Ancient coins found in a strange place

WHERE The Sherman Minton Bridge

COST Free to drive across

PRO TIP Roman coins would have been worthless in Indiana in 238 A.D.; there wasn't even a McDonald's around yet.

Roman coins similar to these were found during the construction of the Sherman Minton Bridge. Public domain photo/ Wikimedia Commons.

discovery of ancient relics in the U.S.—such artifacts have been found from Texas to Illinois. *Weird Kentucky* even notes that coins from the same era were unearthed in a cave in Breathitt County, Kentucky. So, what gives? Did ancient civilizations "discover" North America much earlier than our history would have us believe?

The Sherman Minton is an unusual double-decker bridge, in which the two directions of traffic are one on top of the other rather than side by side.

22 BURGERS FROM A BYGONE ERA

Need a ride uptown? You won't be able to take this trolley.

While Ollie's Trolley originated in Louisville, the tiny restaurants, which literally looked like antique trolley cars painted in bright red and gold colors, spread across the southern and eastern portions of the U.S. after being introduced in the early 1970s by businessman and future Kentucky governor John Y. Brown. They were popular family stops for a time, and it's difficult to track down just how many of them did business in and around Louisville, but they were famous for two things: the Ollie Burger, featuring the secret sauce with twenty-three spices, and the French fries, which were liberally sprinkled with a secret spice blend of their own.

Of course, half the fun was going into the little trolley car, ordering, and then eating in your car or on a nearby bench. Unfortunately, by the 1980s, many of the Ollie's Trolley restaurants were going out of business, and today only a handful remain, scattered across the Southeast. However, one that still operates every weekday from 10 a.m. to 4 p.m. is in downtown Louisville, even though many people seem either to have forgotten about it or

---

Dig around on the Internet and you can sometimes find the secret spice blends for Ollie Burgers for sale so you can make them at home.

One of the last remaining Ollie's Trolleys. Photo by the author.

simply assumed it has closed along with all the others.

Because of its hours, it likely is closed during morning and afternoon commutes through downtown, which may be a reason many assume the restaurant no longer does business. But at lunchtime, there is still often a line out the trolley door. You squeeze in, place your order at a Plexiglass window, then slide to your right to pick up your food in a brown paper bag. That's when the fun begins, because it's hard to beat an Ollie Burger and a side of fries. Don't sleep on this one.

OLLIE'S TROLLEY

WHAT A historic burger joint

WHERE 978 S Third St.

COST $2.10 for an Ollie Burger

PRO TIP Ollie's Trolley is a cash-only establishment.

23 ZOO OF THE DEAD

Why is there a cemetery near the zebra exhibit?

Lions and tigers and . . . corpses? That's right, there is indeed a cemetery in the middle of the Louisville Zoo. The small cemetery, bordered by a stone wall and an iron gate, is the resting place for several members of the Phillips, Durrett, and Clark families. It's an eerie site amid a generally happy, modern atmosphere, particularly given that the cemetery dates to the early 1800s.

A marker, placed there in 1990 by the zoo, explains: "The American branch of the Phillips family began with Jenkin Phillips, born in 1744 in Loudon County, Virginia. He fought with George Washington and helped survey what was then called Kentucky County for Patrick Henry and the Commonwealth of Virginia. For his services, Phillips was deeded one thousand acres of land radiating out from this spot. At the time of his death in 1822, the family owned land extending from this area into southern Indiana."

There is a list on the monument of those memorialized there. But it's off the path just enough that it's easy to walk right by and not notice it at all.

Opened in 1969, the Louisville Zoo currently exhibits more than fifteen hundred animals on 134 acres.

The cemetery in the middle of the Louisville Zoo. Photo by the author.

LOUISVILLE ZOO

WHAT A cemetery in a zoo

WHERE Louisville Zoo, 1100 Trevilian Way

COST $16.25 for adults, $11.75 for kids and seniors

PRO TIP Veer to the right after entering the zoo, then follow the path as it winds back left; keep your eyes peeled, because the tiny cemetery is off the main walking path.

JERRY'S MUSEUM OF ODDITIES

What is all that stuff, and why is it in the middle of a quiet neighborhood?

Jerry Lotz is a collector of odds and ends. His personal collection is on display in the Clifton neighborhood as a sort of public museum, sometimes called the "Art House," and it's nearly impossible to not stop and peruse the assortment of oddities on display. What's odd is that, while it is a neighborhood fixture, many Louisvillians don't even know it's there.

The Statue of Liberty with Richard Nixon's face watches over Frankfort Avenue. Photo by the author.

It seems tough to miss: there's an old train car, plus a train crossing signal. There are vintage cars and gasoline pumps. There are vintage signs and toys. There are clowns, statues, and gargoyles. Facing Frankfort Avenue is a replica of the Statue of Liberty that stands probably ten to twelve feet tall. However, if you look closely, the statue has the face of Richard Nixon, and instead of hoisting a torch, the statue is flashing the "peace" sign.

You may have seen Jerry during a brief appearance on the AMC TV series *American Pickers*, during which hosts Mike and Frank looked through Jerry's stuff and were largely unsuccessful in buying much of it. This is all to say that, if professional pickers can't pry Jerry's treasures away, who can? But looking is free daily.

A peek through the gated "museum" of Jerry's collectibles. Photo by the author.

ART HOUSE

WHAT A suburban museum of weird collectibles

WHERE Corner of Frankfort Ave. and William St.

COST Free

PRO TIP Feel free to feast your eyes on the fun all you want, but please don't touch anything.

Rumor has it the Nixon-faced statue was flashing a different hand signal before the church next door complained.

25 A SECRET CLUB YOU MAY NOT HAVE WANTED TO BELONG TO

What the heck went on underneath Whiskey Row?

Whiskey Row is a legendary part of Louisville that was, a century ago, the nucleus of Louisville's bourbon industry. Distilleries, distributors, and warehouses abounded, and the place was quite the center of activity related to the whiskey industry. Over the years following Prohibition, industry and railroads took over, but later the stretch became home to night life and restaurants.

But in recent years, when the city decided to revive Whiskey Row with retail, residential, and distilling development, a strange and disturbing secret was discovered under the building at 119 East Main: an underground sex club. According to a blog named *The Kentucky Files*, an electrician searching for a live electrical connection amidst discarded whiskey bottles and other rubble happened upon a secret door. He opened the door and followed a set of wood steps two stories below Main Street, only to find a room filled with S&M paraphernalia, torture devices—including a hand-cranked torture rack—plastic mats, and furniture. On one wall, the word "LATEX" was spelled out in black and white ink.

Strange and disturbing murals lined the walls (Salvador Dali? Really?), and the space appeared on the verge of collapse. The discovery garnered international media

Somewhere under this gutted building lies the destroyed remains of LATEX. Photo by the author.

coverage, and no one really knew exactly what to make of the club—until one of the club's former members went to the local media.

"A group of about eight of us decided to form an organization to promote and teach people about safe ways to practice sadomasochism," the unnamed man told WHAS-11 News. "We employed safety personnel and guards to insure nothing dangerous, non-consensual, or untoward ever took place, and to my knowledge never did."

Well, that at least makes me feel better.

A fire ravaged the block a couple of years after the discovery, halting development of the space for many months.

26 LOUISVILLE'S SECRET CONNECTION TO NEW ORLEANS

What is that building façade doing on River Road, anyway?

Many generations ago, Louisville's affluent part of the city was a neighborhood just east of downtown called The Point. As early as the 1840s it was the home of many wealthy people who had relocated from New Orleans, or had simply purchased a home farther northeast to use during hot summer months down south.

But as time went by, the neighborhood also became inhabited by German and Irish settlers, followed by more and more blue-collar citizens, helping give birth to the neighborhood now known as Butchertown. Mansions abounded, including the Heigold House, built by a German settler in the 1850s. However, many of the larger homes were sacrificed during re-routing of Beargrass Creek in the 1850s, and as the neighborhood slowly deteriorated, it became susceptible, thanks to its location so close to the Ohio River, to the devastation brought by the 1937 Flood.

There is a little-used trail that follows Beargrass Creek from Lower Brownsboro Road to the Ohio River, and along some of those pathways are remnants of streets once located in The Point.

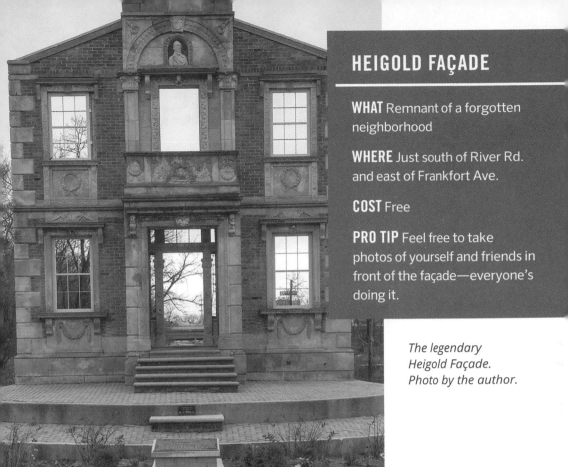

HEIGOLD FAÇADE

WHAT Remnant of a forgotten neighborhood

WHERE Just south of River Rd. and east of Frankfort Ave.

COST Free

PRO TIP Feel free to take photos of yourself and friends in front of the façade—everyone's doing it.

The legendary Heigold Façade. Photo by the author.

Today, only one complete original building remains, and it is situated by the waterfront behind a new residential housing development. Whispers indicated that there are plans under way to turn the building into a restaurant. The Heigold Façade stands just a stone's throw away, overlooking River Road from the foot of Frankfort Avenue, a reminder of The Point's history, even if most Louisvillians today have no idea what the façade represents. The site of The Point later became a dumping ground, but is now being converted into a garden that will be known as Botanica, scheduled to open in 2018. I just love a happy ending.

27 THE REMNANTS OF SHIPPINGPORT ISLAND

Is that land mass in the river just there for the electric company?

There's an island adjacent to Louisville's west end, separated from the city by the McAlpine Locks and Dam, and accessible only by boat or by a tiny white bridge. While the main purpose of the island now is to be home to Louisville Gas & Electric, it once was a heavily populated and developed town called Shippingport.

This island town was home to industry, barge construction, taverns, retail shops, and residential areas. Incorporated in 1785, it at one point had a population of some five hundred people. It was home to Elm Tree Garden, which featured a distillery and horse racing, and it was also home to Jim Porter, the man known as the "Kentucky Giant," who owned a tavern on the island.

Not surprisingly, flooding was a problem, and as the Portland Canal was widened little by little to make way for barge traffic, the island shrank and the population decreased. When the 1937 Flood struck, much of Shippingport was destroyed. The last families left the

---

Shippingport Island is believed to be memorialized in the 1845 song "First of Autumn," with this couplet: "I only hauled but one load instead of hauling four/And got so drunk in Shippingport that I couldn't haul no more."

SHIPPINGPORT ISLAND

WHAT The island site of a forgotten river town

WHERE West End off N. Twenty-Sixth St.

COST Free

PRO TIP To find the park, take West Main to Twenty-Sixth Street across the bridge to Shippingport Island. The public area will be on the left after you cross the bridge.

Top photo, it's a serene scene on the north side of Shippingport Island. Bottom photo, a view of downtown Louisville from Shippingport. Photos by the author.

island in 1958 when the federal government acquired the last remaining private land.

Today, in addition to being the home of LG&E's generators, there is a small public park wherein one can picnic, fish, take a short hike, or just marvel at the smaller islands and scenery on the opposite side of Shippingport overlooking the Falls of the Ohio.

28 SQUIRRELS OF A DIFFERENT COLOR

What odd rodents inhabit the University of Louisville's campus?

The University of Louisville is a fairly typical college campus, which is to say it is mostly students and faculty, with lots of buildings, and with a few oddities. One of those oddities is that the Belknap campus is home to a long-lasting inhabitation of albino squirrels. Employees and students alike see the squirrels going about their squirrelly business, and sometimes they'll capture a photo or two.

It's unknown when the white squirrels took root on the campus, but they are a celebrated feature. For a short time, there was even an active Twitter account with the handle @UofLsquirrel, an account that featured a profile photo of a white squirrel climbing down a tree, and the motto, "I am the University of Louisville white squirrel. I own this campus."

Of course, they're just squirrels, so they don't seem to aspire to any sort of totalitarian empire; they just go about their business, gathering nuts and climbing trees. But they are lovely to behold, and give the campus a certain boost of beauty. Nothing wrong with that.

There are plenty of albino squirrels that scurry around University of Louisville's campus. Photo by Elizabeth Reilly.

ALBINO SQUIRRELS

WHAT Albino squirrels

WHERE University of Louisville Belknap Campus

COST Free (if you can find them)

PRO TIP Bring some unsalted peanuts to share with them. Why not?

The squirrels are so popular that the university's literary magazine is called *The White Squirrel.*

29 IT'S MORE THAN JUST A TRAIN TRESTLE

Does a bizarre, mystical creature haunt Pope Lick?

In Louisville's southwest area, a Norfolk Southern Railway track crosses Pope Lick Road and empties onto a trestle which spans a deep divide. Legend has it that a half-man, half-goat creature lurks there under the trestle, luring unsuspecting victims to their demise.

The Pope Lick Monster is speculated to be anything from an escaped circus freak to a reincarnated farmer who once sacrificed goats to Satan. For decades, visitors to the trestle have reported hearing strange sounds, and many have tried walking across the trestle to investigate in hopes of catching a glimpse of the legendary creature.

The truth is that a number of deaths have been reported at the Pope Lick Trestle over the years, many of them believed to have been people in search of the monster. Is it worth it? There is a 1980s documentary about the legendary beast, which should help satisfy curious thrill-seekers.

POPE LICK TRESTLE

WHAT A haunted train trestle

WHERE South Pope Lick Rd.

COST Free

PRO TIP Be smart. Don't go out onto that trestle. Please.

Look, but don't walk. Photo by fr2002/Wikimedia Commons.

In early 2016, a young woman from Ohio tragically fell to her death from the trestle while in search of the Pope Lick Monster.

30 RADIO STILL MATTERS

Did you know America's first-ever high school radio station launched just across the river from Louisville in 1949?

If you're ever scanning the radio looking for a song you recognize, you may or may not have landed briefly on WNAS, 88.1 FM, the radio station of New Albany High School in Indiana. Launched in 1949, it was the first-ever high-school-sponsored radio station in America, designed as part of the school's journalism and media curriculum. For four decades, the program was overseen by teacher Lee Kelly; the general manager now is Kelly's former assistant, Jason Flener.

Programming ranges from talk to local news to school happenings to sports to music that is programmed by the student DJs, which means you might hear anything from Benny Goodman to the B-52s. It's the kind of free-form media that quite frankly is a dying breed in our increasingly politically correct and commercially-driven society. The radio station begat WNAS TV in 1980 as a video companion station on local cable access.

Above all else, how many radio stations still take requests? WNAS does. Just call the DJ and tell them what you want to hear. Now that's good radio.

Many Louisville radio and TV personalities reportedly consider the WNAS studios better than their own.

WNAS has been broadcasting ever since radios looked like this. Photo by Joe Haupt/ Wikimedia Commons.

WNAS 88.1 FM

WHAT A high school radio station

WHERE 88.1 FM on your radio dial

COST Free, if you own a radio

PRO TIP Call 812-542-4702 to make a request.

31 THE TINIEST SUB-STATION

Why is there a tiny, turn-of-the-century building attached to a parking garage?

There is a tiny, red brick and clay building attached to the side of a multi-level parking garage in downtown Louisville; it houses some valves as part of the infrastructure of Louisville Gas & Electric. But why is it there, stuck to a parking garage? Good question.

Best I can tell from research published on the Internet, the parking garage was built around the little sub-station in the 1980s, as the entire garage structure has an indention the size and shape of the building, which apparently dates to 1919 or 1920, according to the excellent website brokensidewalk.com. The cute little building has been in danger of demolition on several occasions, once when the garage was being built, and more recently a few years back when one of the walls shifted when some workers were doing utility work around it.

Broken Sidewalk referred to the building as a "historic oddity," noting it was originally built without a foundation—making it even more miraculous that it has

---

As recently as 2011, the building was slated for demolition, but it keeps on surviving.

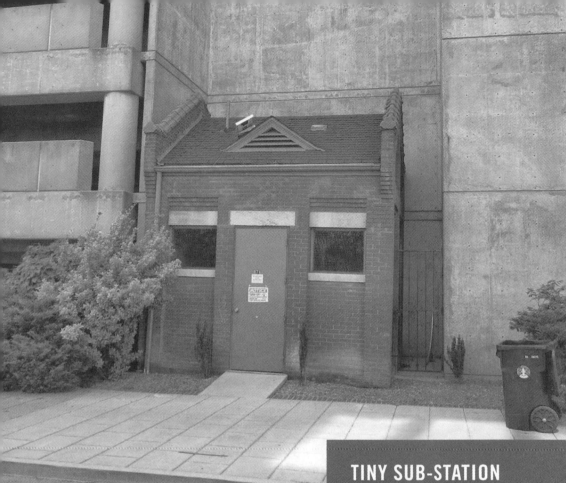

The tiny sub-station looks right at home. Photo courtesy of Eerie Indiana.

survived for nearly one hundred years. We should all be so lucky to last a century; then again, I wouldn't want a parking garage built around me.

TINY SUB-STATION

WHAT A century-old building in a strange place

WHERE Armory Place, just south of Liberty St.

COST Free

PRO TIP The tiny building is located at 1414 Armory Place downtown.

32

THE CHRISTIAN FAMILY CABIN AND CEMETERY

Is that really a graveyard and a log cabin adjacent to a suburban shopping mall?

If you're going to Oxmoor Mall in St. Matthews—a small town/suburb in Louisville's east side that is a retail development monster, with two shopping malls just a stone's throw from one another, and more shopping and chain dining than you can shake a stick at in a two-mile radius—you just might notice the Christian family home and cemetery.

The old log cabin, which now has fantastic access to some great shopping opportunities, originally was built in 1785 and owned by William Christian.

CHRISTIAN FAMILY HOME

WHAT A historic cabin and cemetery in a shopping district

WHERE 7900 Shelbyville Rd. (well, behind it, anyway)

COST Free

PRO TIP If you find yourself at Kohl's, just look at the adjacent lot across from Oxmoor Mall. You'll see the cabin and cemetery if you pay attention.

The old cemetery overlooks the road where shoppers come and go every day. Photo by Cynthia Bard.

The cabin is just a stone's throw from Kohl's and Oxmoor Mall. Photo by the author.

He didn't live there long, as he was killed by Native Americans just a few months later, but his cabin survived. Interestingly, Evan Williams, the bourbon pioneer, was contracted to build a stone fence around the lot's cemetery in 1801.

Another prominent Louisville family, the Bullitts, would marry into the Christian family and many are buried in the cemetery. While the cabin and cemetery are not open to public tours, one can stop and take a quick peek any time.

After you check out the grounds, you can hit Kohl's for some great deals on pants. Beats making your own, which is likely what the Christian and Bullitt families had to do.

33

THIS PLACE IS A ZOO . . . SORT OF

Why are there emus and bison living together on an East Louisville farm?

About ten miles outside of Louisville in Prospect is a hidden treasure that will delight the entire family: Henry's Ark. Set on about six hundred acres of farmland just off S.R. 42, the farm-meets-zoo is buzzing with animals of all types, from ducks to donkeys, ostriches to rabbits. Heck, you might even see a zebra or a camel, if you're lucky.

Basically, you park and enter the pathway between the fences that keep humans and animals separate, and you're welcome to pet the sheep and goats and whatever approaches you. (Be careful, though, because the ostriches might just be after some food.) The great thing is that most of these animals are docile to the point of being domesticated. While some are shy—one little goat peered

A goat sits quietly in his food trough. Photo by the author.

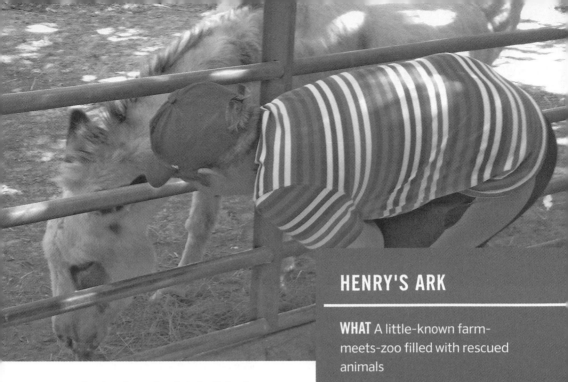

*Petting the animals is half the fun.
Photo by Cynthia Bard.*

HENRY'S ARK

WHAT A little-known farm-meets-zoo filled with rescued animals

WHERE 7801 Rose Island Rd.

COST Free

PRO TIP Please don't feed the animals. Previously, feeding was not only allowed but encouraged, but that practice had to be stopped. (Apparently, some people don't know what to feed an emu.)

at us with pensive curiosity from a tiny wooden house as we passed by—many, such as the donkeys and goats, will walk right up to you. One goat sat sunning himself in one of the many feed troughs, not at all concerned with what any of the other animals thought of him.

It's a fun afternoon for all ages. It's also a cheaper alternative to a public zoo, and arguably just as fun and educational.

Be sure to drop a few dollars into the donation slot as you pass by, as Henry's Ark operates mostly on the kindness of others these days.

34

THOMAS EDISON'S CRASH PAD

What's so special about that tiny little house in Butchertown?

Louisville's Butchertown neighborhood has a unique history, having gotten its name for not only its bevy of butcher shops, but the proximity to meat processing businesses such as the Bourbon Stockyards, dating back to the first part of the 1800s.

But there is another, lesser known, historic footnote to be found in Butchertown in the form of a tiny house where inventor Thomas Edison once lived during the short time he worked in Louisville as a Western Union telegrapher. The tiny red brick structure—a rare, shotgun duplex built around 1850—is a bit off the beaten path, just a block and a half off East Main Street near Shelby Street, and it's so little that it would be easy to drive right by and not notice.

But inside are relics such as early versions of the incandescent light bulb and electrical fixtures, old cylinder and disc phonographs, telegraph machines, an Edison Kinetoscope, photographs, period literature, educational materials, and even a mockup of what Edison's living quarters (dubbed "The Edison Bedroom" by a worker there) might have looked like.

One must wonder if Nikola Tesla, Edison's rival, enjoyed better digs when he was up-and-coming.

The tiny house where Edison once lived is on a side street near downtown and would be easy to miss. Photo by the author.

EDISON HOUSE

WHAT The place where a famed inventor briefly lived

WHERE 729 E. Washington St.

COST $5 for adults, $4 for seniors, $3 for students six and up

PRO TIP The fruit on the mantel in Edison's bedroom isn't real, so don't eat it.

35 WORDS HAVE TO COME FROM SOMEWHERE, RIGHT?

Who coined the term "workaholic"?

You know the person: the type A personality who hyper-focuses on projects, responsibilities, job performance, and the like, while ignoring their sleep, health, and family. Yep, that's what we have for many years now called a "workaholic." Interestingly, that term was coined in Louisville at the Southern Baptist Seminary.

Wayne E. Oates, who wrote fifty-seven books during his adult lifetime (so he would certainly know about being overworked), published *Confessions of a Workaholic: The Facts about Work Addiction*, in 1971, in which he suggested that working exceptionally hard can become addictive, much like alcohol. The catchy, unique phrase became part of our collective lexicon.

Oates lived to the ripe old age of eighty-two, dying in Louisville in 1999, so he didn't work himself to death, but his son, Dr. Charles E. Oates, told the *New York Times*, "My father was just an absolute, bustling dynamo of energy."

Oates' famous book.

Regardless of the fact that he literally wrote the book on work addiction, the author didn't necessarily endorse the workaholic lifestyle. In 1978, he published a book titled *Workaholics: Make Laziness Work for You.* Is there such a thing as a lazi-holic?

DOUBLE YOUR PLEASURE

Who came up with the idea to add flavor to chewing gum?

At a little drugstore at Tenth and Walnut Streets, the latter of which is now called Muhammad Ali Boulevard, a pharmacist named John Colgan had a quandary. The year was 1873, and legend has it that the pharmacist had purchased way more chicle than he needed—a railroad car full of the stuff, to be precise—which led him to an idea. He decided to combine the chicle with balsam tolu extract, which he used for making syrup, and the result was a chewy substance that tasted great. And so, flavored chewing gum was born.

With the help of his son William, the inventor began to market the product as Colgan's Taffy Tolu. Naturally, it was a hit, and Colgan would go on to experiment further, creating gum with longer and longer-lasting flavor. The gum soon was being sold in round metal tins, paired with baseball cards depicting star players of the day, and the popularity led to Colgan selling the Colgan Chewing Gum Company in 1910.

Chicle is a milky substance tapped from the sapodilla tree, by people called "chicleros." It's anyone's guess why someone would buy an entire railroad car of the stuff.

Flavored gum was an invention that revolutionized chewing, in a way. Public domain photo/Wikimedia Commons.

COLGAN CHEWING GUM COMPANY

WHAT Flavored chewing gum

WHERE Tenth St. and Walnut St. (now Muhammad Ali Blvd.)

COST How much is a pack of gum these days, anyway?

PRO TIP If you leave your gum stuck to the bedpost overnight, the flavor might not be so robust in the morning.

Colgan memorabilia is now quite popular with gum collectors (yes, there is such a thing) today, with several people paying as much as $350 per stick to a dealer who had come up with a stash of seventeen original Colgan's Taffy Tolu sticks, according to a Collectors Weekly story from 2011. Apparently, the gum had been locked away in a barn in Chicago since the early 1900s, and even the appraiser wanted to buy the stuff from the lucky collector who found it. Is it fair to wonder if the flavor managed to last one hundred years?

37 NOT AS COMMON AS IT ONCE WAS

Was there really a style of beer invented in Louisville?

Sometime in the mid-1800s, German brewers came to Louisville and began brewing their beloved lager beers. However, a lager beer takes longer than an ale takes to get to market due to the cold fermenting process, so they needed something else to sell. That led unknown brewers to use available ingredients like corn, barley, and rye—the same stuff Kentucky distillers were using to make bourbon—to invent a completely new style of beer. That style became referred to as "common beer" or "common cream ale," and by the latter part of the nineteenth century, some eighty percent of Louisville residents were drinking it on the regular.

Refreshing, light-bodied, mildly tart, and low in alcohol, Common (also sometimes spelled "Komon") truly was the beer for the common man—affordable and attainable at every tavern. Some breweries in town made nothing but Common, because it was profitable. After Prohibition, Common died away, but it still stood as one of only two beer

---

New Albanian Brewing Company, Against the Grain Smokehouse & Brewery, Apocalypse Brew Works, and Great Flood Brewing are other local breweries that have made, or still make, versions of Kentucky Common.

FALLS CITY BREWING COMPANY

WHAT A historic local beer

WHERE 116 S. 10th St.

COST $9.99 for a six-pack, or usually about $4 or $5 for a pint

PRO TIP You'll have to go to the brewery to find it, but the Apocalypse Brew Works version of Kentucky Common, called Oertel's 1912, is brewed using an actual recipe from the era.

Enjoy a taste of history. Photo by the author.

styles to be invented in America. And so, with the resurgence of beer's popularity, so too, has the beer now known as Kentucky Common, resurfaced; Falls City Brewing Company, a brand that actually dates to 1905, reimagined the beer as a flagship brew, and that version is now available in retail outlets by the six-pack. Hopefully this time the beer will stick around; it is the beer the common man deserves.

38

THE HISTORY OF THE JEFFERSONVILLE QUADRANGLE

What was this odd building complex before it became a combination municipal and commercial space?

These days, most people know the odd, semi-horseshoe-shaped structure on busy Tenth Street as the Jeffersonville Quadrangle, but originally it was known as the Quartermaster Depot. When it was built in 1874, it was designed to house Union units stationed in the city, but as the Spanish-American War descended, it was turned into a facility that made uniform shirts for U.S. troops.

These efforts continued through World War II, until finally the operation was shut down in the late 1950s. The fort-like structure, which once featured a watch tower, was used for storage, small businesses, and other such come-and-go operations, as it fell into disrepair. In 1993, a massive fire destroyed part of the old structure, and most believed the complex would be demolished.

During the Spanish-American War, the Quartermaster Depot was cranking out shirts for troops to the tune of about ten thousand per month.

It's a military depot turned shopping center. Photo by the author.

But the city of Jeffersonville decided to purchase and restore it, a process which finally was complete in 2006. Today, it houses several commercial businesses, from restaurants to video design businesses, and a new city hall was built in the center of the courtyard to serve as the anchor.

JEFFERSONVILLE QUADRANGLE

WHAT A former military depot that is now a shopping and municipal center

WHERE E. Tenth St. in Jeffersonville, IN

COST Free to browse

PRO TIP Soak in the history, but also try the hot salsa at Puerto Vallarta. Yummy.

39

AN EYE IN THE SKY

The namesake of the Hubble Space Telescope lived where?

Most people have heard of Edwin Hubble, the famed astronomer who was immortalized by the high-powered space telescope that bears his name. Not everyone knows that as a young man, Hubble briefly lived on Everett Avenue in the Highlands, right after attending undergraduate university in Chicago.

It's true. Hubble's family moved from Chicago to Shelbyville, Kentucky, in 1909, before Hubble returned to Chicago to study law. But his heart wasn't in it. When Hubble's father died in 1913 (he is buried in Cave Hill Cemetery), the young man moved back to the Louisville area with the remaining family, moving into a house at 1287 Everett; the couple also lived for a time at 1318 Brook Street. Hubble took a position as a teacher of Spanish, mathematics, and physics at New Albany High School, just across the Ohio River in Indiana, where he also coached the school's basketball team.

Of course, we all know what happened next: after the passing of his father, Hubble got back to his first love, astronomy, received a PhD in 1917, and became known worldwide for his many discoveries, including proving that

HUBBLE SPACE TELESCOPE

WHAT A surprising local connection to a space telescope

WHERE The Highlands and New Albany High School

COST N/A

PRO TIP If you squint really hard at the night sky, you might be able to see the telescope. OK, not really.

The Hubble Space telescope. Public domain photo/Wikimedia Commons.

Edwin Hubble once lived in Louisville and taught at New Albany High School. Public domain photo/Wikimedia Commons.

the universe was far more expansive than previously believed, with other galaxies existing beyond the Milky Way. NASA's massive space telescope that bears Hubble's name in tribute was launched into space in 1990, where it remains today.

Like anything floating around in outer space, the Hubble Space Telescope will have a shelf life; it is expected to last until approximately 2030 to 2040 before it decays and becomes unusable.

40

FORT DUFFIELD GUARDED THE WEST

Where was Louisville during the Civil War? Caught in the middle . . .

During the Civil War, Louisville was in a precarious position: stuck in the middle. Technically a Southern state, but not exactly beholden to the Confederate beliefs, it found itself in the line of fire from both directions, in a way. As such, multiple forts were built in and around Louisville as a way of protecting the city from invasion.

Positioned along the Ohio River, at the mouth of the Salt River at West Point, Kentucky (just west of Louisville down Dixie Highway), was the Union-held Fort Duffield, a unique earthen fortress in the important position of defending Louisville from attack not only via waterways from the west, but also roadways from the south. The "fort" essentially was a clearing with ten cannons atop a hill, and protective walls fashioned from dirt. Lookouts could see for a good mile in any direction, while cannon fire could reach nearly

The fort as it appears today.
Photo by Figmig/Wikipedia Commons.

The view from Fort Duffield. Photo by Figmig/Wikipedia Commons.

triple that. Many men died of disease at Duffield, and there was one skirmish, but all in all it held its point well, and by 1863 was no longer critical.

Once the war was over, the hillside fort was eventually claimed by nature, and finally awarded to West Point as park space in the late 1970s. It was revitalized, and a replica fort built atop the hill where Duffield once stood. Many of the mounds from the original fort are still visible, and now it is a little-known tourist spot for Civil War reenactments, biking, hiking, and tours, plus special events such as Civil War Days, held each May.

Some believe the fort to be haunted, and nighttime paranormal tours are available—if you dare.

41 THE LEGEND OF SLEEPY HOLLOW ROAD

Is there a spooky black hearse that haunts this rural stretch of country road?

Similar to the Pope Lick Monster legend just southwest of Louisville, the legend of Sleepy Hollow Road warns of spooky dangers that lurk in the night—although this one doesn't involve a half-man, half-goat. Rather, it's a black hearse that seems to come from nowhere.

As the legend goes, drivers have reported driving through the nearly pitch-black canopy at night, and suddenly having a pair of bright headlights in their rear-view mirror. The mysterious vehicle creeps closer and closer, forcing drivers to go ever faster, making the dark curves more and more difficult to navigate. Finally, the hearse pulls alongside and begins to nudge cars off the road and into the hollow some thirty feet below.

That, or a lot of stoned teenagers have overestimated their navigational skills one too many times and used the curse as a convenient excuse. But that's not all: along the way, drivers on Sleepy Hollow Road will pass what is known as "Cry-Baby Bridge," so called because of screams and cries that have been reported from the creek below, which some believe are haunts based on a legend of women throwing unwanted babies off the small bridge. Some legends also say if a full moon shines on the water, one can see shapes of babies' skulls on the water's surface. Others who travel Sleepy Hollow Road by night have experienced time warps, during which several hours pass when it should have only been minutes. That's not to mention the rumors

It's a beautiful drive by day and a potentially scary one by night. Photo by the author.

SLEEPY HOLLOW ROAD

WHAT A haunted road

WHERE Prospect, KY

COST Free, except for the gasoline you burn . . . or potential damage to your car if the legend is true

PRO TIP Go in the daytime, when the sun shining through the tree canopy is beautiful, and spectral hearses are never seen.

of satanic rituals being conducted in the 1970s and '80s at nearby Devil's Point.

I drove Sleepy Hollow Road one afternoon last autumn, and let me tell you, the drop-off is precipitous and scary, even with a guardrail in place. And the tree canopy is such that I could vividly imagine just how dark it gets at night.

Is the haunting real? Well, it bears noting that Harrod's Creek Cemetery is not far away, just east on Highway 329, so it's conceivable that a spectral hearse might take that road. Either way, I'm not going out there after dark, just in case. Travel at your own risk.

The Cry-Baby Bridge legend is one that is common across the United States, so that one may be questionable.

42 SHRINER CITY

What are all those statues of Shriners holding children?

As you drive around Louisville, you may notice statues of a Shriner holding a small child in his arms. The Shriner depicted in the statues, which is titled *Silent Messenger*, is wearing a signature Kosair fez and red bolero jacket, and the child depicted either wears leg braces or uses a crutch (there are two versions). These statues represent tributes to Kosair Charities for ongoing support of local medical research and hospitals, especially for children.

Interestingly, the statues, of which there are now more than twenty, were inspired by a photograph taken in 1970 of Shriner Al Hortman, who in the photo was helping a young girl named Bobbi Jo Wright. According to a 2015 WAVE-3 interview with Wright, Hortman had noticed Wright, who was born with cerebral palsy, was having trouble navigating a playground outing, so he picked her up and carried her from ride to ride.

Finding the statues involves a bit of a hunt, but there are several you can seek out: at the University of Louisville Hospital on Hancock between Chestnut and Muhammed Ali; in front of Home of the Innocents, 1100 East Market Street; at Kosair Shrine Center, 200 South Second Street; and at St. Joseph's Home, 2823 Frankfort Avenue, among others.

If you like the statues, check out the entrance to the Kosair Shrine Center on South Second Street, which is shaped like a giant fez.

THE SHRINER

WHAT A set of unique statues

WHERE All over the city

COST Free

PRO TIP You can find a full list of the Shriner statues and their locations at kosair.org.

This version of Silent Messenger *is one of twenty or so around the city. Photo by the author.*

43 THE CANDY MUSEUM

What's that hiding in the back of the candy store?

Schimpff's Confectionery is a staple of not only Jeffersonville, Indiana, but nearby Louisville as well. Situated on the main drag of Jeffersonville's historic downtown, the sweet shop opened in its current location in 1871, and is still family owned nearly a century and a half later, which boggles the mind. But as you can imagine, it's not really a secret.

But what many forget, or simply miss, is that in the back room of Schimpff's is one of only a handful of known candy museums, featuring literally thousands of pieces of candy memorabilia, from candy tins to vending machines, to toys and advertising. One of the more intriguing artifacts is an early 1900s-era salesman's sample bag, packed with cylinders of various candy samples. The weird part is, the cylinders are still full. I don't even want to know if that's the original candy inside.

There are also photos around the room, flanked by brief histories of various aspects of candy-making culture. As one might guess, anytime children walk into the room, their heads nearly explode with excitement over the many dazzling colors, toys, and signs. Or maybe it's from all the chocolate they ate at the front candy counter. Either way, it's a partially hidden adventure just waiting to happen.

Sometimes, employees will sit in one of the shop's windows facing Spring Street making candy in full view of passersby. How did kids in the late 1800s resist?

There's a candy museum in the back of a candy store. Could life get any better? Photo by the author.

SCHIMPFF'S CONFECTIONERY

WHAT A candy museum hidden in a sweet shop

WHERE 347 Spring St. in Jeffersonville

COST Free

PRO TIP Make your way past the candy displays and soda counter, turn right, and then left again when you see the candy-making line . . . if you can get past all that candy, that is.

COLGATE CLOCK (page 6)

OUR LADY OF LOURDES GROTTO & GARDEN (page 108)

CHICKEN STEPS (page 4)

SPELLS

KENTUCKY SCIENCE CENTER (page 150)

GEORGETOWN DRIVE-IN (page 12)

MEGA CAVERN (page 118)

ART HOUSE (JERRY'S MUSEUM) (page 50)

THE VINTAGE FIRE MUSEUM (page 196)

McALPINE LOCKS AND DAM (page 188)

ST. MARTIN OF TOURS (page 122)

JOE LEY ANTIQUES (page 144)

SAUERKRAUT CAVE (page 190)

44 THE HIDDEN PRAYER GROTTO

Where does one go to find a truly secret place for reflection?

In 1927, the Sisters of Charity of Nazareth, having been relocated from an infirmary downtown to one in the St. Joseph neighborhood between Bradley Avenue and Preston Street, dedicated a small grotto which would be designated for meditation and silent prayer.

The original infirmary is long gone, having been replaced by an apartment complex, but the Grotto and Garden of Our Lady of Lourdes remains, nearly one hundred years later, in part because the neighborhood surrounding the grotto worked hard to preserve it and its history. In 2001, it was designated as a Local and State Historical Landmark, which should keep it around for a good long time.

The grotto is serene, as you would imagine, and quite breathtaking to behold, with its brick boundary, stone walk, ornate sundial, and of course the gorgeously constructed stone altar. There are memorial markers for many, from locals to Pope John Paul II to the "Original Grotto Grannies" who preserved the space. During spring and summer, flowers are always blooming in the grotto, which is just a stone's throw from busy Eastern Parkway. In short, the place is breathtaking.

After you meditate, hit Nord's Bakery or Dairy Kastle for a sweet treat.

The prayer grotto is serene and gorgeous. Photo by the author.

GROTTO AND GARDEN OF OUR LADY OF LOURDES

WHAT A historic hidden grotto

WHERE 4400 Paralee Dr.

COST Free

PRO TIP If you go, turn onto Bradley Ave. off Eastern Parkway, and you'll find the marker outlining the history of the space. From there, you can walk (or drive) down Presidents Blvd. to find the grotto.

45 A HISTORIC DINER

What is that tiny diner in downtown New Albany?

Back in the 1930s, a Wichita-based company called Valentine Manufacturing had the idea to create quick-build diners for aspiring restaurateurs who wanted to open a diner in their town. The Valentine diners were small, usually eight- to twelve-seat structures with a built-in kitchen ready to serve a limited menu to a limited number of people, which made them perfect for a one-person operation.

The diners were a huge hit, spreading all over the U.S. and becoming iconic staples of post-WWII America. As the years went by, the diner craze in America slowly fizzled, and one by one, the Valentine diners followed suit. But some of the diners have held on, one of which is still in operation in New Albany, Indiana, just across the river from Louisville.

The Little Chef was a specific model created in 1957 by Valentine with a distinctive, instantly recognizable design. The one in New Albany not only was a Little Chef model, but for most of its life it was actually called "The Little Chef." It served reasonably-priced breakfast and lunch to locals in downtown New Albany for more than fifty years before an ownership change, followed by a closure.

It was purchased and reopened as a Latin-themed concept called Coqui's Cafe in 2015, then sold again in late

THE LITTLE CHEF

WHAT An original Little Chef diner

WHERE 147 E. Market St., New Albany, IN

COST Under ten bucks if you order well

PRO TIP Note the mini lock-box/safe near the door, a built-in amenity for many of the Little Chef diners.

The Little Chef as it appeared for most of its life in downtown New Albany. Photo by the author.

The Little Chef getting its new paint job in late 2016. Photo by the author.

2016 only to be reopened again as a soup and sandwich place called Lady Tron's. Fifty years in, The Little Chef appears to be nowhere near extinction. Stop in soon for a meat sandwich.

It isn't really known how many Valentine diners such as Little Chefs were built and sold, but one estimate in the late 1940s was that the company had already shipped them to thirty-eight different states.

46 THE HAUNTING OF WAVERLY HILLS

Just how haunted is this place, anyway?

It's no secret that Waverly Hills Sanatorium is believed by many to be a creepy, haunted place, and it stands to reason, as Waverly was born as a place for those suffering from or dying of tuberculosis. So, yes, that oddly shaped building certainly saw its share of suffering and death during its run from 1910 until 1961, when an antibiotic was discovered that cured tuberculosis.

But here's the thing: I have a friend who participated in an overnight Waverly tour. Her report afterward? "Never again." I did a dawn tour many years ago and saw shadow people with my own eyes on the fourth floor; our tour guide reported that one group who spent the night on the top floor in a tent did so cowering in fear from the figures walking around the tent all night. Then again, it all could just be the barometric pressure.

The property owners want to restore the building and turn it into a hotel and convention center, but funding such an undertaking has been slow. Will it ever happen? That's the bigger mystery here. And if it does, will the ghosts move elsewhere?

WAVERLY HILLS SANATORIUM

WHAT A haunted former sanatorium

WHERE 4400 Paralee Ln.

COST $20-$60

PRO TIP It's a fairly long trip from downtown to Waverly, but it's pretty easy—just head out Dixie Hwy., take a left onto Paralee Ln., and follow the winding road around until you see the old sanatorium on the left.

The place even looks like it should be haunted. Creepy. Photo by Kris Arnold/ public domain/Wikimedia Commons.

What many don't know is that Waverly is a historic structure which began not as a hospital but as a school, built in the late 1800s by Maj. Thomas H. Hays, a commander during the Civil War at the battle of Shiloh, along with other notable involvements. He simply was concerned that his daughters had nowhere nearby to get an education. Between that and the role Waverly Hills played as a sanatorium, the truth is that it's a historical landmark as much as it is a haunted curiosity.

47 THE LEGEND OF PAN

Does the Pan statue in Cherokee Park come alive?

Cherokee Park is filled with all sorts of oddities, but the Pan statue atop Hogan's Fountain, which lies along the Scenic Loop across from the cone-shaped Hogan Fountain Pavilion, may be the most intriguing. The fountain itself was sculpted by Louisville artist Enid Yandell in the early 1900s, originally intended as a watering station for horses and dogs, and it has long been a destination spot in the massive park.

Pan, of course, is the Greek god of the wild, shepherds, and flocks; he has the hindquarters, legs, and horns of a goat, which make him a bit on the creepy side right out of the gate. But the word "panic" apparently is derived from Pan's name, which lends to the belief that Pan might be a bit of a troublemaker.

OK, now for the legend: the Pan statue that overlooks Cherokee Park from the top of Hogan's Fountain magically comes to life at the stroke of midnight any time there is a full moon. He then gallivants around the park creating the kind of mischief that only Pan can create. So, during the morning after a full moon, Pan gets the blame

---

On your way to visit Pan, you might see an odd-looking round structure with what looks to be a dragon-shaped boat jutting out. That's what is left of the Christensen Fountain, a memorial to Paulina Keofoed Christensen built in 1901.

HOGAN FOUNTAIN

WHAT A strange statue that comes alive

WHERE Cherokee Park at Hogan's Fountain

COST Free

PRO TIP Just don't park near the Pan statue at night during a full moon, and you'll be fine.

The Pan statue in Cherokee Park comes alive at night, or so the legend says. Photo by Alan Canon/ Wikimedia Commons.

for anything from scratched paint on a car to turned-over garbage cans in the park. Hey, somebody must be doing it, right? Might as well be Pan.

THE LOUISVILLE CLOCK

Whatever happened to that giant clock in the middle of Theatre Square?

Unveiled on Fourth Street in 1976, the Louisville Clock is a unique piece of design that celebrates Louisville's culture. In a sense, it's a forty-foot-tall wind-up toy depicting a horse race in the spirit of the Kentucky Derby. The statue served as a centerpiece for Theatre Square on Fourth Street for many years.

Each day at noon, a bugler would emerge to announce the start of the race, which featured Daniel Boone, George Rogers Clark, Thomas Jefferson, King Louie XVI, and the Belle of Louisville. Unfortunately, almost from the get-go, the clock tended to malfunction. It was moved to make way for a shopping center called the Galleria in 1981, then moved again. And then again.

Finally, in 2011, the refurbished clock was relocated to Theatre Square, where it enjoyed new life—for about four years. Progress being what it is, the space was purchased, and the clock disappeared, possibly for good this time. Best

---

The clock was designed by Barney Bright and unveiled to a group of three thousand people on December 3, 1976.

The Louisville Clock in its heyday. It is now in storage. Photo by Macewindu239/Wikimedia Commons.

I can tell, it is still under wraps somewhere until such time as a new home can be found.

"We have looked at several possible locations," a city official told the *Courier-Journal* in 2015. "Unfortunately, a site remains a hot potato. Everyone loves the clock, but no one seems to have room for it."

LOUISVILLE CLOCK

WHAT A unique mechanized clock

WHERE Semi-permanent storage

COST N/A

PRO TIP The Louisville Clock originally was meant to be much bigger, but budget cuts forced the designer to scale back. At least it's easier to store.

49 THE LOUISVILLE MEGA CAVERN

Bike trails and zip lines underground? But how?

You like adventure? Well, Louisville has a unique adventure for you: the Louisville Mega Cavern, the only underground ropes course, plus a zip-lining course, dirt bike courses, tram tours, secure document storage, and the world's largest underground Christmas lights display. It's a gigantic cavern of fun!

But how the heck did it get there? I mean, really, who digs a hole that big to build a zip line course when you can just build one on top of the dirt? And therein lies the secret. Those caverns were created starting in the 1930s when mining for limestone to build Midwest highways began; mining lasted for about forty years.

Photo courtesy of Louisville Mega Cavern.

The Mega Cavern is just the tip of the iceberg. Photo courtesy of Louisville Mega Cavern.

LOUISVILLE MEGA CAVERN

WHAT A giant cavern

WHERE Beneath the Louisville Zoo

COST Varies

PRO TIP The entrance to Mega Cavern is located at 1841 Taylor Ave.

In the 1960s, during the Cuban Missile Crisis, it was designated as a bomb shelter, with a co-owner of the mine noting that geologists called it "the safest place in Kentucky." But once mining was completed, most of the cavern lay dormant, until current owners came up with creative ways to utilize the space. Amazingly, only a fraction of the four million square feet is currently being utilized. Maybe they can put an entire theme park in there someday.

The Mega Cavern, huge as it is, still is only a part of a series of caverns spanning seventeen miles beneath Louisville.

50 ELVIS'S GRANDFATHER LIVED AND IS BURIED IN LOUISVILLE

Does that mean Elvis used to come here to visit?

Everyone knows about Elvis Presley, revered worldwide as the "King of Rock 'n' Roll," and many remember that Elvis played at the Armory in Louisville in 1956, but did you know that the King's grandfather lived here? He died in 1973 and is interred in Louisville Memorial Gardens.

Born in Memphis in 1896, Jesse D. Presley apparently was regarded as the "bad apple" of the family, and had a reputation for being "mean as hell." Some reports state that Elvis had very little contact with his paternal grandfather, while other legends tell that the performer would, at least in his early career, visit his grandfather here in secret.

What we do know is that Jesse Presley also was a performer of sorts, appearing on the TV show *I've Got a Secret* in the late 1950s. He also recorded a record of his own, which included the tunes, "Who's That Kickin' My Dog Around/The Billy Goat' Song" and "Swingin' in the Orchard." (It's true; you can even look them up on YouTube and give them a listen.)

Legend has it that Jesse D. Presley liked to "drink, dress sharp, and womanize."

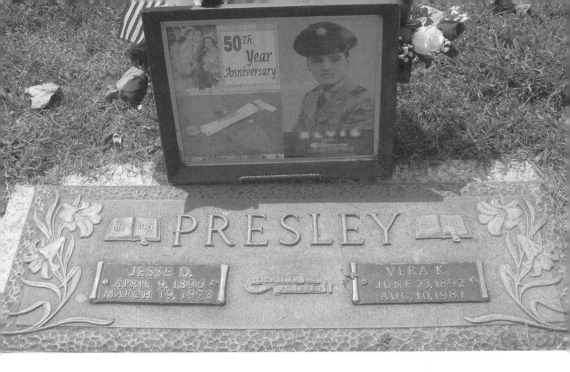

The grave of Jesse D. Presley. Photo courtesy of Bob Cole.

LOUISVILLE MEMORIAL GARDENS

WHAT The grave of the King's grandfather

WHERE 11601 Ballardsville Rd.

COST Free

PRO TIP To find the grave, seek out lot Good Shepherd A1.

51 THE REMAINS OF TWO CATHOLIC SAINTS ARE ON PERMANENT DISPLAY

Wait, those are just really elaborate Halloween decorations, right? RIGHT????

In each side altar in the cathedral at St. Martin of Tours is a glass case, each one containing a human skeleton in full view, wearing robes and adornments. These are the skeletons of St. Magnus, a Roman centurion and martyr, and St. Bonosa, a virgin and martyr, both of whom were put to death by the Roman Emperor Diocletian in 207 A.D. And they are now in Louisville.

The remains lay in the catacombs of Pontiani, Italy, for some fifteen hundred years before being moved into the care of the Cistercian Nuns of Agnani for another two

St. Magnus, a former Roman centurion. Photo by the author.

St. Bonosa at St. Martin of Tours. Photo by the author.

ST. MARTIN OF TOURS

WHAT Skeletons of two Roman saints.

WHERE St. Martin of Tours Catholic Church, 639 S. Shelby St.

COST Free

PRO TIP If you decide to take a look, be sure not to walk in on a mass—the mass schedule is online.

centuries. However, the Italian government confiscated the monastery. Luckily, Pope Leo XIII agreed to turn over the bones to St. Martin of Tours Church. They were shipped to Louisville, arriving here on the last day of 1901, where they have rested ever since.

The relics are here to serve as examples based on their sacrifices; viewing them is a serene and surreal experience. They are open for viewing—just turn off your cell phone's sound and be respectful and quiet.

Every July 15, St. Martin's Church celebrates with St. Bonosa's feast, followed by St. Magnus's feast on Aug. 19.

TAVERN MEETS MUSEUM

Why is there a bicycle hanging from the ceiling of Spring Street Bar & Grill?

From the outside, Spring Street Bar & Grill looks like just another neighborhood tavern. But once you walk inside,

Don't fear the saddle stool.
Photo by the author.

well, you know it's anything but. Sure, it's a place where locals come to wet their whistle, maybe order a dozen of the signature Spring Street wings, or nosh on a Benedictine and bacon sandwich, but while there, it's almost impossible not to marvel at the mini-museum located within.

From local beer memorabilia like old chalk statues, bottles, and signs, to the antique bicycle (I think Pee Wee Herman is still looking for this thing), what looks to be an old rocking horse, a couple of rifles, and an old baby carriage, you're liable to find just about anything and everything. Of course, there's the big "Whiskey" sign that lights up the front

There are two barstools near the bar that are topped with leather saddles—it's like riding a horse, only less smelly, and with no saddle sores.

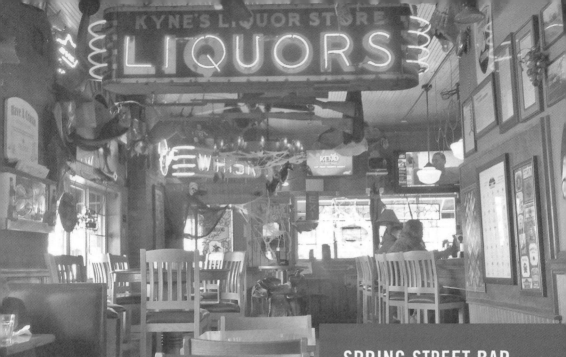

Spring Street Bar & Grill is a fun place to grab a sandwich and a cold beer. Photo by the author.

part of the bar, which is in a constant showdown with the front end of some unidentified car from the 1950s mounted to the opposite wall. In between, the old sign from Kyne's Liquor Store tries to act as mediator.

And of course, there are worse ways to spend time than simply sitting at the bar with a beverage and a snack, enjoying the huge ornate bar, complete with an arched mirror trimmed in a floral design.

SPRING STREET BAR & GRILL

WHAT A tavern filled with curious treasures

WHERE 300 S. Spring St.

COST Free

PRO TIP Spring Street Bar & Grill wings are legendary, and are super cheap on Mondays.

53 IROQUOIS PARK'S HEADLESS HAUNTING

Does a headless woman haunt Iroquois Park?

The Overlook at Iroquois Park is a beautiful and serene place where one can overlook the Ohio River and downtown Louisville from the 250-foot knob. It's especially beautiful at sunset and is a popular place for couples or families to spend a couple of hours enjoying the scenery.

But per legend, the park—and especially the area around the Overlook—is haunted by a headless woman. If you're ever at the Overlook after dark, and a mist rolls in, it might be time to go. If you then hear footsteps coming toward you, it's definitely time to go. She will appear in 1800s-era clothing, carrying her bloody head in her hands, blood trickling from the stump of her neck.

OK, so sightings of the headless woman are few and far between. But the 725-acre park, which opened in the early 1890s, is truly an out-of-the-way treasure designed by Frederick Law Olmstead—who designed Central Park in New York and much of Louisville's park system—to be "a scenic reservation of forested hillsides and breathtaking vistas." Heck, all of Louisville's parks are like this, which is just one amenity that makes Louisville a great place to live, ghost or no ghost.

In addition to the popular Overlook, the park, which was imagined as "Louisville's Yellowstone," also features an amphitheater, a golf course, picnic areas, and more.

The Iroquois Overlook. Photo by Retired_Username/Wikimedia Commons.

THE OVERLOOK

WHAT A park overlook with a strange mystery

WHERE 5216 New Cut Rd.

COST Free

PRO TIP As long as you're there, you might as well enjoy the sunset.

THE FORGOTTEN HIGH RAIL

Did you know there was once a high rail transit system in Louisville?

If you've ever been to Chicago, you've no doubt ridden "the El," the elevated, electric train line that takes commuters from north to south and all points in between. The elevated track runs all through the city, having become an integral part of the Windy City's landscape.

Believe it or not, Louisville used to have one of those. The relatively short-lived Louisville elevated train system spanned a total of about ten miles, and a portion of Louisville's trains were electric even before Chicago's line (although for a few years they were pulled by steam engines). Researcher R. David Schooling extensively studied Louisville's mostly forgotten El system. In an article on brokensidewalk.com, he notes that the system featured waterfront platform stops at First, Fourth, and Seventh Streets from about 1893-1907, after a steam-powered version was in operation from 1886-1893.

The system was designed for quicker transit, turning what might be a thirty-minute ride on the city's streetcars into a ten-minute jaunt overhead. A portion of it ran

---

The iconic train station at Seventh Street and River Road, roughly where the Muhammad Ali Center sits now, became home to Actors Theatre of Louisville.

Union Depot, Louisville

THE EL

WHAT A forgotten electric train line

WHERE Formerly right above your head

COST N/A

PRO TIP Next time you drive along I-64 downtown, you can roughly imagine what it was like looking out over the Ohio River from the window of an El train.

A postcard depicting the train station at Seventh Street. Public domain photo.

along the Ohio River where Interstate 64 is today, went into New Albany via the K&I Bridge ("the Daisy Line," as it was known) and into Jeffersonville via the Big Four Bridge (now a walking bridge), "radiating out like spokes on a bicycle wheel from downtown," Schooling wrote.

Of course, as automobiles became more and more prevalent, train usage dwindled. Eventually, the lines— electric and steam—stopped running altogether. Few people remember the trains now, as they exist mostly in scattered photographs and historical documents.

55 THE LOST UNDERGROUND ROLLER RINK AND BOWLING ALLEY

Did you know there was once a roller skating rink and bowling alley in the basement of a local shopping center?

In 1962, the Mid-City Mall opened in the Highlands neighborhood sporting twenty-two new stores in a square-ish building, promising not just a new shopping experience but family entertainment value as well. In the basement level of the single-story mall were a skating rink and a bowling alley, perfect for entertaining the kids while mom shopped for clothing.

More than half a century later, the mall is still open but the rink and alley are long gone. Mid-City Mall now sits in the middle of a heavily-traveled night life and dining scene, and as such has added a comedy club, a bar, and a movie theater to its offerings. In the basement, one piece of history can still be found: the skating rink— which is now the Nearly New Shop—is relatively intact, much as it was more than fifty years ago.

The former bowling alley space now is home to a gym called Jim Cain's Mid-City Fitness; things lifted there are heavier than bowling balls.

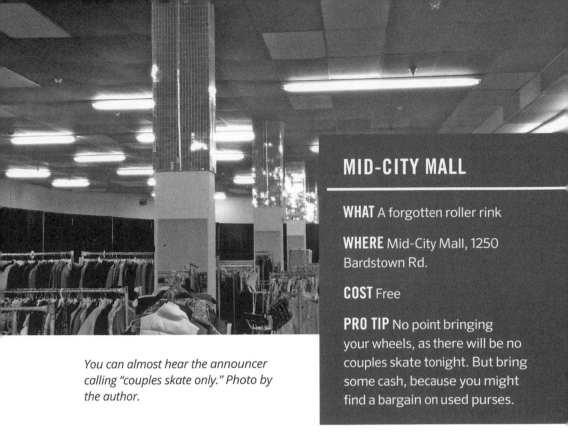

MID-CITY MALL

WHAT A forgotten roller rink

WHERE Mid-City Mall, 1250 Bardstown Rd.

COST Free

PRO TIP No point bringing your wheels, as there will be no couples skate tonight. But bring some cash, because you might find a bargain on used purses.

You can almost hear the announcer calling "couples skate only." Photo by the author.

The place even smells like the past, and as you walk into the store and through the area that once likely was occupied by a snack bar and tables for kids to congregate, you can begin to see the columns around which junior high schoolers skated laps. Step down to the next level of the store, and you're on the wooden track itself, which still creaks like every old, wooden skate track seems to do. In fact, walk around a bit and you'll almost feel uncomfortable that you're *not* sporting roller skates.

Topping the columns are disco-style mirrors, which most certainly appear to be original, as does the multi-colored, festive-looking drop ceiling. And one can almost hear the sound of the skates as they roll across the planks, and the chatter of kids who have long since passed into adulthood. Hey, and there are plenty of dresses and purses, if you're looking for bargains.

56 THE WITCHES' TREE

Did witches of long ago place a curse on this gnarled tree?

This unique-looking maple tree at the corner of Sixth Street and Park Avenue is startling to look at no matter how it came to be so gnarled and grotesque. But the back story is even weirder than the tree itself.

As the story goes, during the late nineteenth century a coven of witches would gather there to perform ceremonies, until a city planning committee decided to cut the tree down for a May Day celebration, angering the witches and prompting them to cast a curse.

Less than a year later—actually, eleven months to the day—the city was hit with a storm so severe that it actually caused locals to fear the witches had called forth a "storm demon" (a phrase which made the local headlines), unleashing damaging storms on the city. During the storm—and this is lore, mind you—lightning struck the stump of the old tree, and a new tree began to grow. A tree that looked like . . . well, just look at that thing.

Whether the legend is true or false, the tree is something to behold, although it's advisable to be polite and not mess with the offerings. You just never know.

Today, people bring signs, dolls, witch balls, crosses, horseshoes, and other offerings to hang in the tree's branches, either to pay homage to the witches or to appease them.

THE WITCHES' TREE

WHAT A cursed tree

WHERE At the corner of Sixth and Park Streets

COST Free

PRO TIP Might be best not to disturb the tree. Just in case.

People still place tributes to the witches on the tree.
Photo by the author.

57

CHURCHILL DOWNS ALMOST DIDN'T SURVIVE

Did you know the world's most famous race track almost had to close?

If you've been paying attention, you know that Churchill Downs is pretty much the epicenter of thoroughbred racing and has been for generations. It is home of the Kentucky Derby and Kentucky Oaks and the destination of countless tourists, celebrities, and racing enthusiasts hoping to cash in on a longshot.

But the now-legendary track was a financial bust at first, and changed ownership multiple times before it finally began to turn a profit in the early 1900s. Horse racing had experienced a surge in popularity in the early to mid-1800s, but interest had begun to wane by the time the first race would be run at what would become Churchill Downs. That in itself might have prevented it from existing, had not two other horse tracks, Oakland and Woodlawn, recently closed, creating a void.

Col. Meriwether Lewis Clark, grandson of famed explorer William Clark, founded the Louisville Jockey Club, which opened the following year. In 1937, the track was officially renamed in honor of Clark's uncles John and Henry Churchill, who owned the land on which the track sat.

In the early 1900s, new ownership sought to soften its reputation as a gambling venue by adding a social aspect in the form of concerts, fairs, steeplechases, and other events. One event that took place there involved two train locomotives crashing into each other head first as spectators

A photo of how Churchill Downs looked in 1901. Public domain photo/ Wikimedia Commons.

looked on. All of this helped to foster more interest in the track, likely saving it from financial instability and helping pave the way for a legend that continues to grow.

CHURCHILL DOWNS

WHAT A historic race track's secret

WHERE 700 Central Ave.

COST Varies

PRO TIP The first Saturday in May in Louisville might be reserved for mowing the lawn if not for Churchill Downs.

The mint julep didn't become the signature drink associated with the Kentucky Derby until 1938, around the time the current name was made official.

58

AMERICA'S LARGEST VICTORIAN NEIGHBORHOOD

Is Old Louisville America's most haunted neighborhood?

With forty-five square blocks and more than fourteen hundred old homes featuring classic architecture from the late 1800s, Old Louisville is well known as one of America's largest Victorian neighborhoods, complete with a central fountain and park, numerous shaded walking courts, and layers upon layers of nineteenth-century charm. In addition, the money and history that has bubbled up from this neighborhood is almost breathtaking—in fact, Old Louisville also has been called one of America's "most architecturally exuberant neighborhoods." In other words, Louisville spared no expense.

Many Louisvillians neglect the neighborhood as they go about their busy suburban lives, but it's worth two hours of your time to simply park and walk around, admiring the architecture and the serenity, or to take a guided walk with Louisville Historic Tours. And if you're feeling a little spooky, author David Domine's walking tour bills Old Louisville as "America's most haunted neighborhood," and he should know—he's written three full books about Louisville's hauntings.

Don't miss Old Louisville. Take the tour. Just don't wander off by yourself.

The historic and gorgeous Conrad-Caldwell House. Photo by the author.

One of the Old Louisville hauntings exists in a mansion known as the Conrad-Caldwell House, allegedly haunted by the Caldwell family. The family purchased it in 1905 and lived there for thirty-five years. Stories of tour visitors wandering off and being confronted by the ghost of Mr. Caldwell abound.

59 FORGOTTEN HISTORY OF THE K&I BRIDGE

What was the original purpose of that dilapidated railroad bridge west of Louisville?

For most, the Kentucky & Indiana (or K&I) Bridge, spanning the Ohio from West Louisville to New Albany, Indiana, is a little-used eyesore on the river. But in fact, it is a bridge of historical significance that as recently as 1979 was still used for vehicular traffic. Once upon a time, it was a bustling thoroughfare for pedestrians as well as horse and wagon traffic.

The bridge is now closed to suburban traffic, but the central part of the structure is a single railroad track, and it is flanked by a pair of wagon ways, with unique metal screening designed to help prevent passing trains from spooking horses. The bridge also features a unique rotating span built to allow tall ships to pass through. But its main purpose was to better connect the two sides of the river—a concept which, from a social perspective at least, seems to escape local residents to this day— representing the first span of the Ohio in Louisville specifically built for pedestrian traffic in a city dominated by far less efficient ferry services.

If that isn't enough, it is aligned with the Great Buffalo Trace and Wilderness Road, where early Americans crossed the Ohio as they migrated westward. The bridge's location is historic for its placement, which helped extend that western movement.

Sadly, the public thoroughfares were closed in 1979 when a truck that apparently was overloaded caused part of the steel grate to sag. Fearing safety issues,

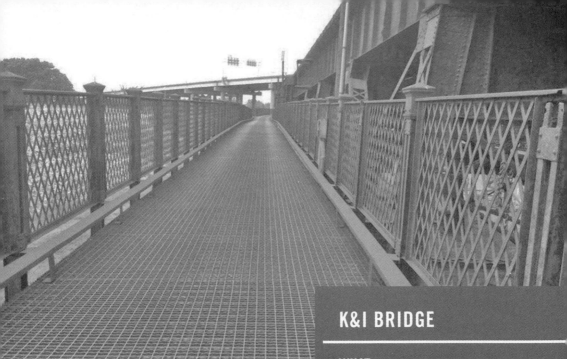

A view of one of the lanes reserved for horse and wagon traffic on the K&I Bridge. Photo courtesy of Eerie Indiana.

K&I BRIDGE

WHAT A bridge that is more than meets the eye

WHERE Spanning the Ohio from Portland to New Albany, IN

COST N/A

PRO TIP One day, you might get to ride your own horse and buggy across the K&I. Or at least ride your bike.

the bridge's owner decreed that both directions of the bridge wagon ways be closed permanently. There has been some momentum in recent years to reopen them for foot traffic, but it's anyone's guess when or if that might ever happen. Nevertheless, the history lingers on.

Louisville's mostly forgotten elevated rail system was for a time attached to the K&I Bridge.

THE SEEDY MYSTERIES OF THE SEELBACH'S RATHSKELLER

Did Al Capone leave behind a twisted mystery?

The Seelbach Hotel (now called the Seelbach Hilton) has roots that date back to 1869, but the current hotel

A view of the Rathskeller as it was being built in the early 1900s. Public domain photo/Wikimedia Commons.

is a magnificent piece of architecture and Louisville history built in the early 1900s. And while some of the hotel's sensational and sometimes dark past isn't necessarily a secret, per se, it's still worth mentioning here just to keep reminding ourselves that it really still exists.

During Prohibition, many of the country's most notorious gangsters gathered at the Seelbach's bar; Al Capone himself had a favorite alcove in the hotel's legendary Rathskeller, a gorgeous subterranean ballroom space filled with ornate columns and design. Capone had a huge mirror brought down from Chicago and placed near his preferred spot so he

Keep your eyes peeled for the Blue Lady, the ghost that roams the Seelbach.

A photo of the Rathskeller as it looks today, set up for a private event. Photo by the author.

SEELBACH'S RATHSKELLER

WHAT A mysterious subterranean ballroom

WHERE The lower level of the Seelbach Hilton, 500 S. Fourth St.

COST Free to see if you ask nicely, but renting it is another matter

PRO TIP The Rathskeller is reserved for private events these days, but if you approach the hotel desk and ask to see it, there's a good chance you'll get your wish.

could watch his back. What's more, there are hidden doors in the room that led to secret passageways so that he could get in and out unnoticed. F. Scott Fitzgerald, who wrote about the Seelbach in *The Great Gatsby*, famously got kicked out of the place for being drunk and disorderly.

But even without the literary and organized crime connections, the Rathskeller is just one weird place; it just has a feel, which is lost on those who only hear about it and never set foot inside. Do some reading, and you'll learn some of what's happened inside the space and what still exists there. At first glance, it looks like it could have been a cathedral. But don't be caught off guard, because the menacing pelicans are watching.

Yes, that's right: pelicans. *Unusual Kentucky*, which investigates such eerie places quite successfully, noted that "the pelican is regarded in some occult mythologies as a symbol of resurrecting one's children after having killed them oneself, by anointing them with one's own blood." Nice. But there are so many strange markings and designs that it's hard to get a grip on what the place is supposed to be. This is just part of what makes it so mysterious.

61 THE BARREL-SHAPED ICE CREAM STAND

What's that red and white barrel and why is there a playground next to it?

It was 1994 when Mark Beam was laid off from his job. The company offered business classes to laid-off employees to help them move forward, which inspired him. His make-believe business for class was an ice cream shop, and once the course was over, rather than seek new employment, he and his wife Lisa decided to open the ice cream stand he had envisioned. That's how Barrel of Fun Ice Cream, located in southeastern Louisville, was born.

The stand features a hard-to-miss, twelve-foot-tall barrel painted in red and white stripes with a pair of order windows. The Barrel of Fun serves up the usual fare: cones, sundaes, milkshakes, flurries, banana splits, and of course burgers and hot dogs. This makes for not just a great summer neighborhood stop, but a rather unique out-of-the-way tourist destination which must be reached by going through a European-style traffic circle. And there's a small playground and plenty of picnic tables for those warm summer days.

Owner Mark Beam told *Louisville Magazine* he believes the barrel structure, which used to be on wheels, was originally a hot dog station used on Long Island, possibly called Barrel of Buns.

Barrel of Fun is out of the way, but worth the drive. Photo by the author.

BARREL OF FUN ICE CREAM

WHAT A unique ice cream stand

WHERE 9421 Smyrna Rd.

COST Ice cream cones start at about $2.50

PRO TIP It's closed October through March (I found out the hard way), so be sure to visit during warm-weather months.

Beam bought the barrel-shaped contraption at a car dealership in a stroke of great timing and good luck, turning it into a local classic in the Okolona neighborhood of Louisville. At the end of the season, in September, Barrel of Fun offers pumpkin-flavored ice cream, and there's even a board outside where you can stick your head through a hole and have your pic taken with a barrel, a monkey, and a curiously big banana. Hard to beat this for family fun.

JOE LEY ANTIQUES

Am I wrong, or does this place feel like more than just your average antique store?

The three-story Joe Ley Antiques is a mainstay on Market Street. Photo by the author.

Featuring literally two acres of antiques, Joe Ley is a Louisville treasure in the heart of downtown. It might not be a "secret" to anyone, but the history of the place sure escapes many, which is why I've included it here. (Well, that, and it's just an amazingly fun place to visit.)

The bizarrely decorated antique shop is set in a three-story "normal school" built in 1860; it was a state-of-the-art school in its day, designed for training school teachers. After the school closed in the 1960s, the building changed hands a few times, then sat boarded up until Ley acquired it just over fifty years ago.

The grounds are gated and the building is surrounded by all manner of statues and other odds and ends, with a distinctive mural on the west side of the building that can be seen a couple of blocks away. Inside, it is part sprawling antique store, part museum. One must pick up a shopping key in order to decode the prices—nothing is priced in dollars and cents, only by code (apparently, it's an inventory thing).

Expect to find everything from skeleton keys to doors to bizarre imported antiques to furniture to clowns to

The old building is packed with fun offbeat antiques and collectibles. Photo by the author.

toys to—well, pretty much let your imagination run wild, and it was all collected by affable owner Joe Ley. Stock is always rotating. What amazes me about the place is the number of doors, mantels, railings, hardware items, and such—you could almost build your own vintage home with stuff from inside this antique store.

Note: I spent the night in the building one time about fifteen years ago because the old structure is believed to be haunted. I didn't see any spooks, but I did run across a couple of cold spots on the second floor, so be prepared.

Joe Ley Antiques has been a supplier for restaurants and for movie props, and has even been used as a backdrop for music videos, movies, and commercials.

63 HAPPY BIRTHDAY TO US ALL

What's so special about those little buildings in the woods?

Listed on the National Registry of Historic Places, the Little Loomhouse and surrounding buildings make up a weaving and textile education center, dedicated to teaching and preserving the legacy of Lou Tate, a master weaver with connections to two American presidents. Morphing from limestone quarry offices to summer homes to an artisan cultural center, the cabin became the home of Tate, who was instrumental in developing the smaller table loom which was named after her.

The loom came about in response to a request by President Herbert Hoover's wife for a way to involve Mrs. Hoover's main interest, the Girl Scouts, in simple weaving projects. This later attracted the attention of Eleanor Roosevelt, who launched Tate into the public eye when she included Tate's weaving school in her syndicated column, My Day. Mrs. Roosevelt later commissioned work from Tate for display in the White House. Somewhere

---

The Hill Sisters, Mildred Jane and Patty Smith, who had a summer cabin nearby, wrote the song we know today as "Happy Birthday to You." Originally titled "Good Morning to All," it was first sung at what is now the Little Loomhouse.

The Little Loomhouse grounds stand as a piece of Louisville history. Photo courtesy of Little Loomhouse.

LITTLE LOOMHOUSE

WHAT A historic weaving preservation and education center

WHERE 328 Kenwood Hill Rd.

COST Varies

PRO TIP Frank Lloyd Wright once visited Little Loomhouse while in Louisville for a convention.

along the way the main cabin was named Esta, which is said to be an old Norse saying meaning, "May God's presence be in this dwelling." The name still is visible on the cabin's door.

The little compound still sits in its original spot, tucked in a wooded area off Kenwood Hill Road, and still offers classes, workshops, and lessons on spinning and weaving. Of course, many zoom right by each day, possibly having no clue of the historical significance of what they're passing.

SECRET COLLECTIONS OF THE MAIN BRANCH LIBRARY

What else would be in a library besides books?

The Louisville Main Branch Library downtown opened in 1908 with books—lots and lots of books. But what many don't know is that the library also had a few other, um, odd artifacts back in its early days. The book "Libraries and Lotteries: A History of the Louisville Free Public Library," published in 1944, reveals a fascinating history of the library, including items kept there that most definitely were not books.

For one, the library had a collection of 1,300 butterflies and moths. And a taxidermized moose head. Even more interesting than that, the library housed a collection of rare bird's eggs. The problem is that many of these oddball artifacts were damaged or destroyed when the Great Flood of 1937 submerged much of the library under water. Perhaps the most unusual item that was damaged by the flood was a 2,600-year-old Egyptian mummy known as Then-Hotep. (Then-Hotep

---

The statue of Abraham Lincoln outside was partially submerged, but survived the Great Flood of 1937. Today, passersby rub Lincoln's toe for good luck.

The Louisville Main Branch Library has been home to more than just books. Photo by the author.

LOUISVILLE MAIN BRANCH LIBRARY

WHAT A secret history of odd artifacts

WHERE 301 York St.

COST Free

PRO TIP In 1950, the Louisville Free Public Library became the first library in America to launch its own FM-radio station. WFPL still broadcasts today, along with sister station WFPK.

was rescued and later came to rest at the Kentucky Science Center.)

Rare birds, Medieval weaponry, Indian artifacts, rare artwork, and more suffered through the flood. What was saved ended up in other spots around the city and beyond. But the history remains.

65 A WAYWARD DINOSAUR IS STILL KICKING

Why is there a gigantic Triceratops in that parking lot?

Talk about having been all over the place—and winding up in a most unlikely place—there's a statue of a triceratops in Louisville that went from being on display at the 1964-65 New York World's Fair, to being in a zoo, then a museum, then to being relegated to storage in an industrial lot, far from the eyes of most anyone around.

The thirty-foot-long, blue-gray statue was part of the Sinclair Dinoland exhibit in New York fifty-plus years ago, an attraction in which children could not only gaze on models of triceratops, brontosaurus, tyrannosaurus rex and others, but also could have plastic statues of the dinosaurs molded and made while they watched. Sometime during the 1970s, the triceratops model came to Louisville, spent some time at the Louisville Zoo, and then became part of the Louisville Museum of Natural History and Science. When the museum shifted its focus and became known as the Kentucky Science Center, the statue was relegated to storage at the out-of-the-way

---

The other dinosaur statues from the Dinoland exhibit are scattered across the country, many still on display, except for Ornitholestes, which was stolen and never found.

The triceratops is weathering with age, but still a sight to behold. Photo by the author.

Great Northern Building Products, located off West Broadway.

So many kids grew up seeing the triceratops around town that it's rather a shame to see it languishing in that lot. But if you have a few minutes, it's not too difficult to find, and it might make your favorite youngster's day to know that, yes, there are dinosaurs in Louisville.

KENTUCKY SCIENCE CENTER

WHAT A dinosaur statue with a surprising history

WHERE 901 S. Fifteenth St.

COST Free

PRO TIP The statue is on the right side of the building (as you face it), and is a bit tough to see from outside the fence, but during regular business hours, the main gate should be open.

66 THE HUBCAP LADY

What's that weird statue in the middle of an industrial district?

The Hubcap Lady, as she often is called, is a huge metal statue built in the early 1980s, accompanied by a giant balance scale and a poem telling her story. The statue, which doesn't appear to be constructed of hubcaps, but rather sheets of molded metal (although they reportedly were indeed once hubcaps), is actually called *Mother*. Her wings flow behind her, an outstretched hand clutching a single flower as she gazes skyward. And she stands next to a railroad track in a mostly unseen industrial district.

I remember driving past the statue dozens if not hundreds of times over the years, always thinking, "What the heck is that thing?" and then completely forgetting its existence until the next time I drove by. I imagine most do the same. So, it was more than interesting to stop and see it up close, to read the poem, and to then do some research into what the statue means. Apparently, the Hubcap Lady is representative of the virtues of women everywhere.

The poem, titled "The Lady" and carved into a wooden sign, reads in part, "I am your mother/Yet I am a woman/Standing into the winds of change/Expected to

---

The Hubcap Lady is part of a two-piece installment—the nearby scales loosely symbolize that love outbalances all else.

HUBCAP LADY

WHAT A curious metal sculpture

WHERE 1275 Dutch Ln. in Jeffersonville, IN

COST Free

PRO TIP Be sure to read the poem on the wooden sign located next to the statue.

The Hubcap Lady, in all her glory. Photo by the author.

be strong/Yet gentle/Expected to be better than good/ Yet not reflect/That I know I am good. . . . Take my hand/ We will stand together/Into the winds of change."

It's quite a moving piece of art, and well worth experiencing—and not at all difficult to find. Just watch out for trains.

A HANDY TRADITION AT HAUCK'S

What are those people doing with those sticks?

Hauck's Handy Store has been a tradition in the Schnitzelburg neighborhood of Louisville since 1912, a classic grocery store with a residence above it owned and operated by a German family. It is a reminder of a bygone era in Louisville. Whereas the store once relied on the staples of bread, meat, flour, and various sundries, today it's more of a stop for lottery tickets and snacks. But it is still owned by the Hauck family, specifically George Hauck, whose mother originally opened the store.

Mr. Hauck is a beloved neighborhood treasure who has helped carry on another tradition in Louisville: a traditional German street game called Dainty. This unique game involves players taking turns to see how far they can hit a stick using another stick. The dainty, a stick about five inches long with pointed ends, is placed on the ground, and the player tries to hit one of the pointed ends with the bat to make the dainty pop up into the air. The player then sees how far he or she can hit the dainty with the bat.

In 1971, Mr. Hauck, now in his upper nineties, created the World Famous Dainty Contest, which happens each summer, with the streets around Hauck's Handy Store

---

The neighborhood is called "Schnitzelburg" because its early inhabits were primarily German; schnitzel is a classic German dish.

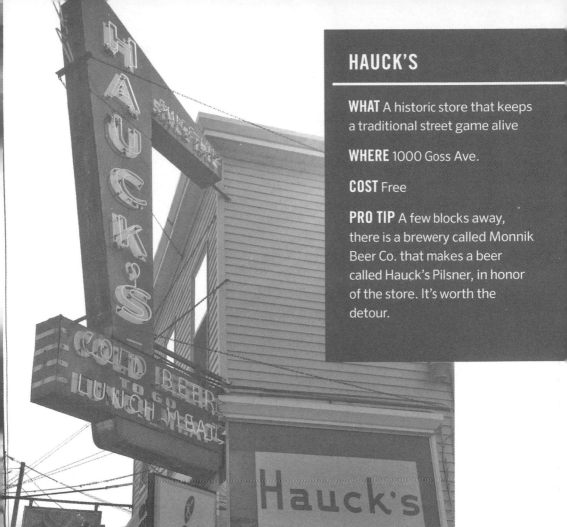

Hauck's Handy Store is still thriving in Schnitzelburg. Photo by the author.

closed off, and people from all over the neighborhood and beyond coming to play, watch, eat, drink, and be merry. Mr. Hauck is always the honored guest, and he wouldn't miss it for anything because it takes him back to his childhood in the neighborhood.

"I have nothing but happy memories," Hauck told me. "Nowadays you have to be off the street. Nobody trusts children being out. Years ago, nobody had any money, but we played street games."

<u>68</u> A LIBRARY OF FIRSTS

Did you know the West Louisville library branch has a special history?

Louisville has a pretty impressive free public library system, with eighteen branches all over the city, from downtown to the far southern reaches of Dixie Highway, but one branch has an important, unusual, and often untold history. The Western Branch Library, as it is known, first opened in 1905—as the first library in the U.S. focused on services for African-Americans, and staffed solely by African-Americans.

Then Central High School principal Albert Meyzeek feared his students did not have enough reading materials at their disposal, so he convinced the city to build a library to help his students, who were mostly African-American. He made history in the process, and the library is still in operation today.

Speaking of which, after the death of flamboyant singer-songwriter, Prince, it was revealed by the Louisville Free Public Library that the musician, by way of his Love 4 One Another Charities foundation, had donated $10,000 to the library in 2001, helping to save it from closing. The donation had been kept a secret by library

LOUISVILLE FREE PUBLIC LIBRARY

WHAT A historic and important library and landmark

WHERE 604 S. Tenth St.

COST Free

PRO TIP The Blue papers also have been digitized and can be viewed at the Kentucky Digital Library website.

The Western Branch Library is steeped in history. Photo by Nyttend/Wikimedia Commons.

officials for the years leading up to his passing.

Local activist Haven Harrington III was the one to break the news via Facebook, adding, "He didn't want people to know. He just wanted to do the right thing without a lot of fanfare and accolades."

The library branch was led for many years by Rev. Thomas F. Blue, the first African-American to head a library. His writings and teachings are now on display at the branch in the recently added African-American Archives Reading Room.

69

ABRAHAM LINCOLN'S GRANDFATHER

Did you know our sixteenth president's grandfather was murdered and buried in Louisville?

Years before Abraham Lincoln was born, his grandfather Abraham Linkhorn (Lincoln) settled in east Louisville in 1781, near what is now Long Run Road. A military captain during the American Revolution, he also was an early settler of Louisville. A tanner by trade, following the Revolution he moved from Virginia and began farming on an estimated fifty-five hundred acres of land, living as part of a colonial settlement.

However, the land was a parcel local Native Americans still considered their own. In May of 1786, while working the fields with his three sons, he was shot dead by someone in the nearby forest. The youngest son, Thomas, stayed by his father, while the other two went for help. One of the sons observed from a distance a Native American emerging from the woods and walking toward his father's body, then reaching for Thomas, so he shot the man dead. It is generally assumed the elder Lincoln was shot by the Native American. Thomas would name his son Abraham, and that son would become the sixteenth President of the United States.

ABRAHAM LINKHORN LINCOLN

WHAT A surprising local connection to U.S. history

WHERE Long Run Baptist Cemetery

COST Free

PRO TIP The cemetery is located on the spot of not only Linkhorn's cabin, but also his murder.

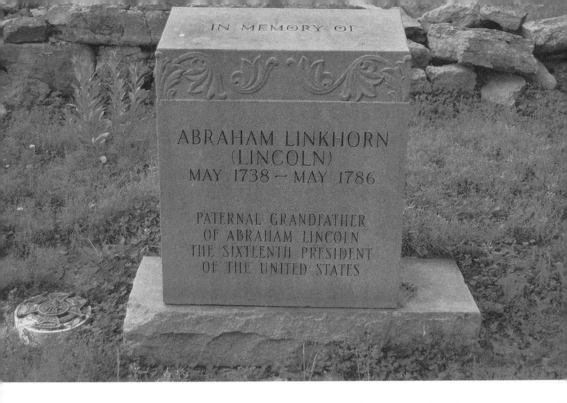

Abraham Lincoln's grandfather finally got a grave marker in 1937. Photo by Nyttend/Wikimedia Commons.

Buried next to his cabin, Abraham Linkhorn didn't get a grave marker until 1937. The spot is now the site of Long Run Baptist Cemetery, and it is accessible to the public.

While he later relocated north and represented Illinois as a Whig party leader, Abraham Lincoln was actually born in Hodgenville, Kentucky, about sixty miles southeast of Louisville.

70

LOUISVILLE'S LITTLE-KNOWN CONNECTION TO THE WORLD'S LARGEST SPELLING BEE

Did you know the Scripps Spelling Bee has roots in Louisville?

And now for a little history that few Louisvillians seem to know about: the first National Spelling Bee, held in Washington, D.C. in 1925, was sponsored in part by Louisville's the *Courier-Journal*. In fact, the now-famous spelling bee wasn't sponsored by Scripps-Howard until sixteen years later. That doesn't mean the first one was any small deal—the nine finalists who competed in Washington got to meet President Calvin Coolidge.

Fittingly, the winner of the first National Spelling Bee was an eleven-year-old boy named Frank Neuhauser, from Louisville, Kentucky (which no doubt explains the sponsorship). He won by spelling "gladiolus," a type of

---

Louisvillian Neuhauser later became a successful lawyer, and would remain connected to the spelling bee into the early 2000s before his death at age ninety-seven.

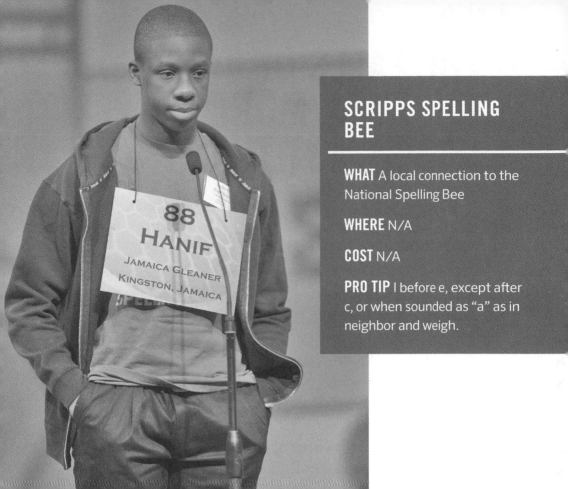

SCRIPPS SPELLING BEE

WHAT A local connection to the National Spelling Bee

WHERE N/A

COST N/A

PRO TIP I before e, except after c, or when sounded as "a" as in neighbor and weigh.

The Scripps National Spelling Bee is still going strong more than nine decades later. Photo courtesy of Scripps National Spelling Bee/Wikimedia Commons.

flower he had raised all his life, which was quite the fortunate stroke of luck for him after Edna Stover of New Jersey whiffed on the word by replacing the "I" with a "y."

Anyway, Neuhauser not only won $500 in gold pieces, he also returned to Louisville to a parade and bouquets of gladiolus, as well as a free bicycle for his triumph.

71 THE FALLS OF THE OHIO ARE MORE IMPORTANT THAN YOU THINK

Isn't it just a bunch of fossils?

If you live in the Louisville area, you know about the Falls of the Ohio, and the 380-million-year-old fossils there. You may even know that the entire area was once the bottom of a vast ocean, which is how those fossils got there in the first place.

And of course you also know the Falls is where Lewis and Clark met to begin their expedition westward, an important event in American history. That was no accident; the waterfall there was a well-known navigational point. But the next time you visit the Falls of the Ohio State Park in Clarksville, Indiana, to walk around on the fossil beds and enjoy a spring day, it's worth considering for a moment just what that naturally-occurring waterfall did for Louisville.

You see, that natural falls made traveling all the way down the Ohio a near impossibility without portaging to the lower level. What does that mean? That means it became a

The Falls of the Ohio State Park Interpretive Center recently underwent a massive redesign, and is well worth visiting to learn more about the importance of the Falls.

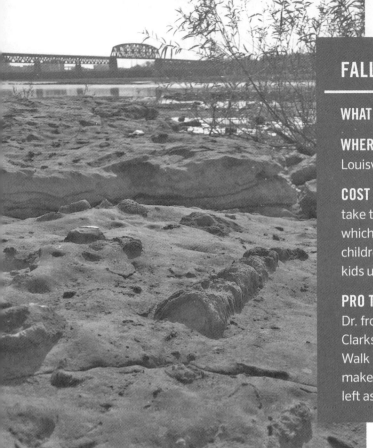

The Falls of the Ohio mean more to Louisville than just fossils. Photo by the author.

natural stopping point, meaning it was also a natural point for settlements to accumulate. As river traffic increased, so did the need for people, labor, resources, supplies—you get the idea. If those falls had been located one hundred miles downstream, we'd all be living in Evansville right now. But we're not, and what we wound up with was a history of building steamboats and barges, a history of being on a major U.S. trade route, and a history of enjoying the proximity of a natural resource most people don't have in their backyards. Don't even get me started on the importance of limestone.

Louisville all too often takes the Ohio River—and the Falls of the Ohio with it—for granted, but these resources truly define who we are.

72 THE SPORT OF KINGS STARTED IN THE STREETS

Was horse racing always the sport of the upper classes?

Horse racing in Louisville begins and ends at Churchill Downs, right? Um, wrong. In fact, what many don't know is that horse racing in Louisville may date back as far as the late 1700s and began as a sport that took place in the streets—kind of like drag racing, except without all the exhaust fumes (although the horses no doubt littered the streets in other ways).

Obviously, there were injuries to both horses and riders alike, not to mention this was already a busy thoroughfare not conducive to such activity, which would eventually prompt race organizers to get a bit more formal. This led in the early 1800s to the opening of race tracks like Elm Tree Gardens, located on Shippingport Island, and Oakland Race Course, both of which predate the opening of Churchill Downs in 1875. Many private farms also held races during the 1800s, while a few other small race courses also came and went before Churchill Downs was established.

Some of these early horse races reportedly happened near downtown on Market Street, which today is a busy thoroughfare known for its restaurants and art galleries in its east sector.

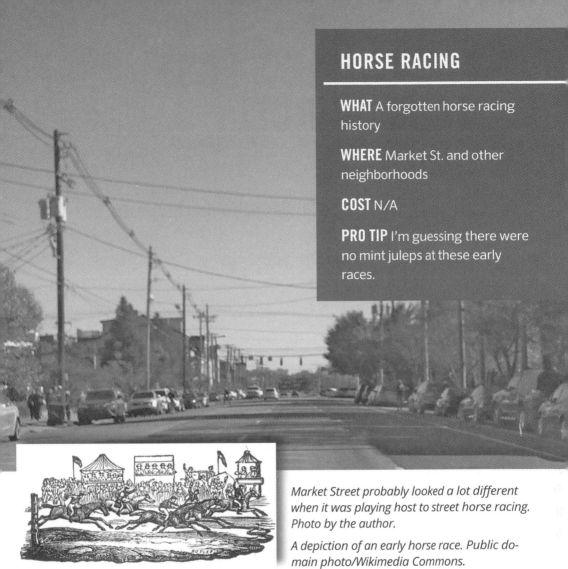

HORSE RACING

WHAT A forgotten horse racing history

WHERE Market St. and other neighborhoods

COST N/A

PRO TIP I'm guessing there were no mint juleps at these early races.

Market Street probably looked a lot different when it was playing host to street horse racing. Photo by the author.

A depiction of an early horse race. Public domain photo/Wikimedia Commons.

The contrast of what these early races must have been like, compared to what we now know as Churchill Downs, is astonishing to consider. No doubt even the most prominent races at Elm Tree Gardens were never celebrated with a celebrity-studded party like the Barnstable Brown party that is attached to the Kentucky Derby. And did Oakland Race Course have a Millionaires Row in 1850? Probably not. At least no one had to look at all the awful hats, though, right?

73 LOUISVILLE'S LOST ROCK 'N' ROLL HISTORY

Did you know Louisville was a thriving music city in the 1950s and 1960s?

It was 1964, and a new hit called "Look Homeward Angel" by a rising young doo-wop band called the Monarchs was climbing the Billboard charts. It was on the cusp of the British invasion, and although American rock 'n' roll was still trying to find itself in the wake of the tragic deaths of Buddy Holly, Richie Valens, and the Big Bopper, the future of pop looked bright.

Of course, few today know that Louisville at the time was on the verge of becoming a true American rock 'n' roll city, thanks to bands like the Monarchs, and the legendary Sambo Studios, located at 9912 Taylorsville Road (there is now an apartment complex on the site). In 1965, Soul Inc., another Louisville band that recorded at Sambo, got the call to tour with Dick Clark's Caravan of Stars. Many other local bands, such as the Carnations, Cosmo and the Counts, and the Sultans, brimmed with next-level talent, including future Louisville music

---

At one point in the 1960s, Louisville was trying to fashion itself as the next Motown.

legends like guitarist Wayne Young and drummer Marvin Maxwell.

Sambo began as a booking agency before building a studio in a non-descript house in nearby Jeffersontown, which would operate for years recording artists of all genres, eventually under the name Allen-Martin Studios before finally moving out of town and later folding. But in recent years, the Sambo tapes have been resurfacing, as nostalgia for Louisville's lost music scene is rekindled by a new wave of music talent fueled by the success of artists like My Morning Jacket and Wax Fang.

ROCK 'N' ROLL

WHAT Louisville's connection to rock 'n' roll

WHERE 9912 Taylorsville Rd. (originally, at least)

COST N/A

PRO TIP Even more modern acts such as Days of the New recorded at legendary Allen-Martin Studios.

74

THE "OTHER" CAVE HILL CEMETERY GRAVES

What famous people are buried here?

Everyone in Louisville knows that Col. Harlan Sanders and Muhammad Ali are buried in Cave Hill Cemetery. The same goes for Pappy Van Winkle, whose line of bourbon is among the most popular in the U.S. or even the world.

But there is much to see in the 296-acre cemetery that sometimes goes unnoticed, like the grave of magician Harry L. Collins, who spent much of his life performing his tricks while promoting Frito Lay, or the parrot, Pretty Polly, which is the lone animal buried in the cemetery.

George Rogers Clark, the famed Revolutionary War leader, is buried there, and one shouldn't miss the gorgeous columned monument at the grave of Florence Satterwhite. James Graham Brown, builder of the famed Brown Hotel, is buried in Cave Hill. Patty and Mildred Hill, composers of the melody to "Happy Birthday to You" are interred therein, as is James Colgan, inventor of flavored chewing gum.

Nicola Marchall, who created the Confederate

Cave Hill National Cemetery, located on the grounds at Cave Hill, is home to the Thirty-Second Indiana Monument, the oldest Civil War memorial in the country.

The grave of Harry L. Collins. Photo by the author.

uniform and flag, rests in Cave Hill, and Jim Porter, the jockey-turned-giant who ran a tavern on Shippingport Island, also rests there. You see where I'm going with this—pack a lunch and spend an afternoon looking for these interesting graves and monuments.

75

A MOSTLY FORGOTTEN LOCAL "FREAK"

Did you know a major Hollywood director was born in Louisville?

Born to a well-to-do family (and the nephew of baseball great Pete Browning), Tod Browning, born Charles Albert Browning, was something of an odd child who was fascinated by the circus and carnival life. At age sixteen, he left Louisville and his family to perform in carnival acts, one of which was as "The Human Corpse" with Ringling Brothers Circus.

But he had higher aspirations, and would later become a filmmaker, directing such classics as *Dracula*, starring Bela Lugosi, among dozens of other films. True to his lifetime devotion to the bizarre, his films followed dark paths, often focusing on the strange goings-on in behind-the-scenes circus life. Perhaps his signature film is *Freaks*, a story in which a high-wire performer marries a dwarf performing in the same traveling circus to steal his substantial inheritance.

Louisville native Tod Browning. Public domain photo/Wikimedia Commons.

The high-wire performer, who is "normal" unlike the "freaks" who surround her, finally openly mocks the collection of actual sideshow performers—which included performers from a set of real-life conjoined twins named Daisy and Violet Hilton to Frances O'Connor, born with no arms and no legs—and the "freaks" take revenge, turning her into a freak like them. Unfortunately, the shocking film was deemed too disturbing to release, and even after significant editing, it mostly spelled the death knell for Browning's directing career (it was even banned in the U.K. for decades).

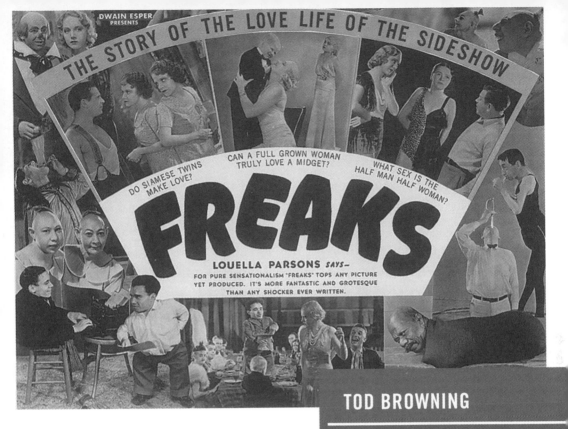

THE STORY OF THE LOVE LIFE OF THE SIDESHOW

DWAIN ESPER PRESENTS

DO SIAMESE TWINS MAKE LOVE?

CAN A FULL GROWN WOMAN TRULY LOVE A MIDGET?

WHAT SEX IS THE HALF MAN HALF WOMAN?

FREAKS

LOUELLA PARSONS *says—*

FOR PURE SENSATIONALISM "FREAKS" TOPS ANY PICTURE YET PRODUCED. IT'S MORE FANTASTIC AND GROTESQUE THAN ANY SHOCKER EVER WRITTEN.

Movie poster for Freaks. *Photo by Employees of MGM/Wikimedia Commons.*

Browning died in 1962, and was buried in California. Sadly, many in Louisville don't know about his Hollywood legacy, let alone his connectioan to Louisville, as no memorial for him here exists.

TOD BROWNING

WHAT A legendary Hollywood director from Louisville

WHERE Hollywood by way of Louisville

COST N/A

PRO TIP You can find *Freaks* and other Browning films on Netflix and online.

Tod Browning's *Freaks* inspired punk band the Ramones to write the song "Pinhead," released in 1977. The song borrows dialogue from the film, including its familiar "gabba gabba hey" chorus.

76 THE WEIRD, SEMI-PRIVATE BATHROOM

Do you see what I see?

On Louisville's bustling West Main Street is a luxury hotel called 21c. In the main floor lobby-cum-art-gallery there is a men's restroom that might just be the weirdest restroom in the entire city. Why? First of all, there is an old-fashioned trough, a creation that has mostly been replaced by modern-day urinals across America.

But the real kicker is that when you, er, step up to the plate to take a swing, you are facing a see-through mirror—which means you have full view of everyone walking down the hallway just a few feet away. No, people can't see in (try as many might) while you complete your business, but . . . well, let's say it can be disconcerting if you aren't accustomed to it. Let's face it, a man's business is a private matter, which is why there is an unwritten no-talking policy in men's rooms across the country.

But to be able to see people of all ages and genders

Trough-diving used to be a sport for the inebriated at Chicago's Wrigley Field, based on Internet footage. Trough-diving is frowned upon at 21c.

21C BATHROOM

WHAT A curious men's room

WHERE 21c Museum and Hotel, 700 W. Main St.

COST Just your dignity

PRO TIP You can always use the stall if you're, um, shy.

You can see out in the 21c men's room, but people can't see in. Thank goodness. Photo by the author.

walk by and glance at you, just knowing what you're doing in there, is truly a unique experience. That is, unless you make it a habit of doing your business in public. I don't need to know.

77 THE STREET WITH FOUR (OR FIVE, OR SIX) NAMES

Does this street ever end?

One street in Louisville is possibly the most confusing in the city. I said "possibly." But if you've traveled from Germantown to the Highlands, or vice versa, you already know which street I'm talking about: Virginia/Oak/Winter/Grinstead.

Looking at a map, it goes something like this: from just east of Interstate 264, Virginia Avenue (which is actually Hale Avenue on the outer part of the loop expressway, though a one-way detour sort of eliminates it from being a separate name change) becomes Oak Street at South Twenty-Sixth, then continues on as Oak until it crosses Interstate 65, then bears left until you get to Barret Avenue. At that point it becomes Winter Street. A couple of blocks away, suddenly it is Grinstead Drive, which is one of the major thoroughfares through the Highlands neighborhood.

But there's one problem: most of that stretch is one way going in the opposite direction. And if you head west from Grinstead, you end up getting diverted onto Mary Street, and then to East St. Catherine and—look, just find a better route. This is why they built the interstate system.

This is a view of the street of many names as you look down Oak. Wait, or is this Winter? No, Oak. Probably. Photo by the author.

VIRGINIA/OAK/ WINTER/GRINSTEAD

WHAT A street that never seems to end

WHERE Virginia Ave. to Grinstead Dr. (or vice versa)

COST Just your sanity

PRO TIP Make sure your GPS is working properly.

If you're driving down Oak Street as part of challenging this weird stretch of road, stop for some Southern cuisine at Southern Express or The Seafood Lady.

THE WITCHES' CASTLE

What is that old stone structure off Utica Pike?

The Witches' Castle, located just across the Ohio River in Utica, Indiana, was a well-known legend as I was growing up; the summarized version is that the old stone structure was the former home of three sisters who cursed the place after they were cheated out of their land around the turn of the nineteenth century. But I had never read the full history until recently, and the eye-witness accounts of the time are disturbing, to say the least, with the sisters being physically dragged from their space, tied up, and placed on a makeshift raft to float downriver to the Falls of the Ohio to their death as townspeople along the way watched.

A blog called *The Accidental Spook* perhaps sums it up best: "Bloody, beaten, and trapped on the raft, town folk recalled watching the sisters struggling and wailing helplessly, when, without warning, all three sisters suddenly froze, their bodies becoming unnaturally stiff. . . . The sisters, moving as if they were one, slowly lifted their heads in unison and glared intently at the vigilantes and gawking town folk, their eyes unnaturally wide and full of hate. Then suddenly, as if possessed, their bodies started shaking with rage and the sisters, raving maniacally, spewed curses and

---

Death found the Witches' Castle once more in 1992, when Shanda Sharer, a local twelve-year-old girl who was tortured and burned alive by classmates, spent her last night on earth with one of the stops during the girl's night of horror being the Witches' Castle.

The Witches' Castle in Utica, Indiana. Photo courtesy of Eerie Indiana.

obscenities at the witnesses on the shore, damning them all and their descendants. For over one hour the townspeople morbidly watched as the raft slowly floated out of sight, the sisters' curses fading in the distance until they were heard no more."

Yikes. Anyway, what's left of the structure still stands, and has been the object of fear and wonder ever since. The town of Utica, which hoped to become a featured Ohio River hub, fell on hard times after the "eviction." Weirdly, three more sisters later moved into the place and were believed by locals to be witches, with children going missing near the property before a raid on the "castle" unearthed evidence to support their misdeeds: human skin, small bones, and what appeared to be a human heart simmering in a pot over a fire.

Why the crumbling castle hasn't completely been torn down is a mystery. Perhaps the curse lingers, and no modern human wants to stir it up again.

79 MR. BONZ RIDES AGAIN

Is that mysterious Jeep traveling around Louisville being driven by a skeleton?

Mr. Bonz is a skeleton. Who drives a car. All over the streets of Louisville. To say that he gets some stares would be an understatement. The back story is that when car enthusiast Andrew Johnson came across a Jeep Wrangler on a car lot that had the steering column on the right-hand side, European style, he thought, "Oh man, I can do something with that."

Enter Mr. Bonz. Asked how he came up with the name for the skeleton who leisurely holds a faux steering wheel and often wears wigs or costumes, Johnson credited his kids. Suffice to say, the macabre motorist gets plenty of attention and stares wherever he goes.

"I literally cannot go anywhere without people asking about him," Johnson says. "If I'm not driving the Jeep, people ask me why I'm not. If I take him out of the Jeep, people asked me where he is. I really don't own the Jeep; he does—it's his Jeep."

MR. BONZ

WHAT A skeleton that drives a Jeep

WHERE All over the road

COST Free

PRO TIP This guy never uses his turn signal, so if you see a bloody Jeep Wrangler, use caution.

Mr. Bonz has Toonces the Driving Cat beat by a mile. Photo courtesy of Andrew Johnson.

Several hundred right-hand-drive Jeep Wranglers are built each year, and are available through dealerships. Skeleton sold separately.

THE HIDDEN CEMETERY OF CHARLESTOWN

Is that a graveyard in an industrial complex?

Finding the abandoned Barnett Cemetery wasn't as easy as I'd planned, since it had been described as "plainly visible" from S.R. 62 in Indiana, just a handful of miles north of Louisville. But I'd probably driven that stretch a thousand times in my life and never seen anything that looked like an abandoned cemetery. And so, I drove right past it, making stop after stop without the benefit of a map.

Finally, a friendly man in a guard shack handed me a map of all the cemeteries that lie within the grounds of the Indiana Army Ammunition Plant, a now defunct facility that made and tested ammunition for WWII and beyond, beginning in 1941. Of course, when the plant was built, the government didn't want to disturb the dead, so there are ten—count them, ten—known cemeteries on the property, portions of which have recently been converted to a commercial industrial business park known as River Ridge Commerce Center. Much of the rest is now a state park.

The Barnett Cemetery contains the graves of some of Clark County, Indiana's, earliest settlers, including Capt. John Blizzard and his family. Most of the graves there tell the exact number of years, months, and days the person lived.

The cemetery over-looks busy S. R. 62 near Charlestown. Photo by the author.

The grave of Capt. John Blizzard. Photo by the author.

BARNETT CEMETERY

WHAT An abandoned cemetery

WHERE The former grounds of the Indiana Army Ammunition Plant

COST Free

PRO TIP If you're driving down S.R. 62 toward Charlestown and you see the 4-H Fairgrounds, you've gone too far. Look for Autoneum North America; the cemetery is on a small hill just west of it, accessible by Patrol Rd.

The most interesting of these cemeteries (to me) is the aforementioned Barnett Cemetery, which dates back to the first half of the nineteenth century and is enclosed only by a hand-made wall of rock. It contains maybe two dozen graves and has been abandoned for decades—and yes, it is visible from the state highway, if you know where to look. In fact, when you stand in the tiny, serene cemetery, with industrial development all around, you can watch traffic go by, oblivious to the history so close by. It's a peaceful and surreal experience that should not be underestimated.

81 A HAUNTING AT THE PALACE THEATRE

Does the ghost of a former employee haunt Louisville's legendary theater?

There's nothing so "secret" about the Palace Theatre (also known as the Louisville Palace)—it is one of Louisville's favorite and most historic entertainment venues, known for its distinctive vertical sign and signature Spanish Baroque motif. So many acts have performed at the Palace (as Louisvillians call it), from Tom Jones to Prince, that it boggles the mind. Of course, it was designed as a movie theater, which was its main purpose for the first five decades of its life, and it served Louisville well.

But what locals may not know is that the Palace is believed by many to be haunted by a former engineer who worked there. According to the Louisville Ghost Hunters Society, workers in the venue who were part of a 1990s renovation to bring it to its current state of restoration began seeing an older man around the place wearing work clothes and out-of-style glasses. One saw the man sitting in the balcony; another worker had fallen asleep on a scaffolding and awoke with a start when a voice whispered "wake up" in his ear—potentially keeping him from falling off the scaffolding as he slept. Other odd occurrences

The Palace still offers a film series, usually featuring classic older films, which reconnects it with its roots.

182

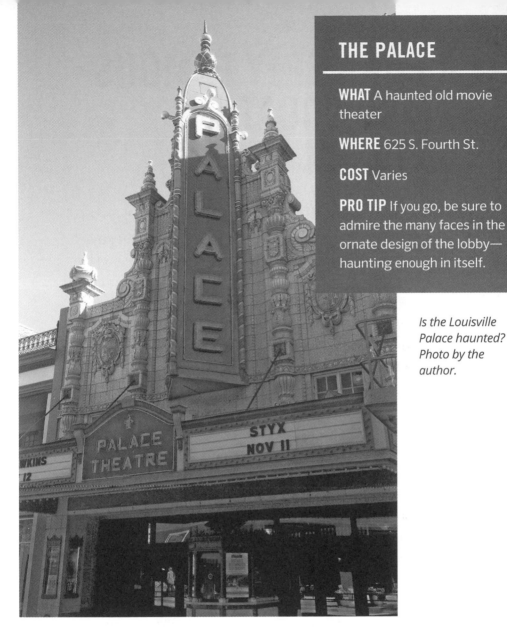

Is the Louisville Palace haunted? Photo by the author.

had Palace owners and employees wondering just what was going on.

Eventually it was learned that a man named Ferdinand "Fred" Frisch had died of a heart attack in the basement of the venue in 1965 after having worked there for some forty years. A photo of Frisch that was uncovered looked surprisingly like the man workers have seen, with the same glasses, hairstyle, and clothes. Does Mr. Frisch still wander the halls of his long-time workplace in a spectral form? No one knows for sure.

A FORMERLY FAMOUS RIVER LOCATION LIVES ON

What is that old farmhouse on the river?

I was paddling down the Ohio River in a hand-built kayak with my friend David during the summer of 2016, and he asked me if I'd like to take a break. We were on the second leg of a fifty-mile journey, so my answer was a quick and resounding "yes." He said, "We can stop at Farnsley-Moreman Landing." I'd heard of the place, but had never been, so he began to regale me with its history.

Farnsley-Moreman Landing was a place where riverboats traveling downstream to St. Louis, New Orleans, or wherever, would stop to trade goods, gather supplies, or simply to rest and have a meal. The three-hundred-acre plot was a famous spot along the Ohio River that was a flourishing center between 1820 and 1890. There also was a ferry there which carried people and goods back and forth across the river daily.

While there is still a landing of sorts at Farnsley-Moreman, it is sadly no longer used. During our trip downstream, David and I simply paddled ashore, sneaked under the chains blocking the stairs up to the grounds, and

---

A small chapel on the site is used often for weddings, while the grounds can be rented for receptions. The chapel, however, is not an original part of the landing.

The stately Farnsley-Moreman farmhouse at the landing. Photo by Joe Schneid/ Wikimedia Commons.

FARNSLEY-MOREMAN LANDING

WHAT A historic old river landing

WHERE 7410 Moorman Rd.

COST Varies

PRO TIP Take the Gene Snyder Freeway west, and it will basically lead you right to the old landing.

looked around. Just watch your step if you find yourself floating downstream and decide to stop; it's plenty muddy and slippery. It is easier to get there by car.

But it's worth the stop—the pre-Civil War brick farmhouse has been lovingly renovated plus the grounds have been restored to what they probably looked like while the landing was in its heyday, with a small chapel added for weddings. Meanwhile, ongoing archaeological excavations promise more discoveries that will further inform Louisvillians about the history of this nearly forgotten landing.

83 LOUISVILLE'S HISTORY OF TATTOOS

You mean there's more here than just ink?

Louisville loves its tattoos—it's quite a tattoo-friendly city, with ink shops dotting the Highlands bearing fun names like Artfully Insane, Twisted Images, and The Monkeez Uncle. But probably the best-known tattoo parlor in town is none other than Tattoo Charlie's, which has been adding ink to skin in Louisville since 1973.

But there's more to Tattoo Charlie's than meets the eye—at the main location in Preston Highway in South Louisville, this tattoo parlor also sports one of America's largest tattoo museums that is available to the public. The museum includes everything from vintage design patterns to antique temporary tattoo sheets, signs, ads, literature, equipment, and more.

I decided to stop in and check it out at opening on a Sunday morning, figuring it would be slow. Well, I was way off—it was like going to the DMV, with people packed in, waiting their turns in chairs. One young woman was asleep on the floor. I tiptoed my way around, checking out the tattooing artifacts as the others chose their tattoo patterns and waited to get inked up. It all makes for a pretty cool spectacle, with all you ever wanted to know about tattoos there in one place.

Tattoo Charlie's is the best-known tattoo parlor in the city, in part because of its amusing slogan, "Tattoos while you wait."

Tattoo paraphernalia of yesteryear abounds at Tattoo Charlie's. Photo by the author.

TATTOO CHARLIE'S

WHAT A tattoo museum

WHERE 7904 Preston Hwy.

COST Free

PRO TIP Original owner Charlie Wheeler's son Buddy now owns the small chain of tattoo shops; the museum comprises his collection of memorabilia. Feel free to ask for him and say hi.

84

LOCK IN, LOCK OUT

What exactly does that lock thing in the river do?

The McAlpine Locks and Dam is something of an unnoticed engineering marvel that motorists drive past every day without giving much consideration to. It has been a critical part of Louisville's success since it was first opened in 1830. Why? Because the Falls of the Ohio, as historically meaningful as they are, also are something else: a massive natural barrier to river traffic.

MCALPINE LOCKS AND DAM

WHAT Historic locks and dam on the Ohio River

WHERE 805 N. Twenty-Seventh St.

COST Free, if you're in a boat

PRO TIP You can paddle your canoe through the locks to get an idea of just how massive they are.

In a book called *Triumph at the Falls: Louisville and the Portland Canal,* authors Chuck Parrish and Leland Johnson wrote of the Falls, "Here, the river fell twenty-six feet over jagged rocks, cascading down in impassable whitewater rapids." Beautiful, yes. Practical? No. It meant waiting for a flood to even the drop or portaging around, a grueling process.

And so came the modern marvel of the locks and dam, designed to accommodate barges and boats heading east or west, using a mechanical, self-powered structure that was designated a Historic Civil Engineering Landmark in 2003. Every day, countless craft go through the locks—each of which is roughly the size of three football fields combined—ensuring that vital river traffic can move past the Falls with minimal trouble.

Locking through McAlpine in a canoe or kayak can be an intimidating experience. Photos by the author.

There is an annual September event called the Mayor's Hike, Bike & Paddle in which hundreds of canoes and kayaks paddle through the locks at one time; it is truly a disarmingly humbling feeling to be inside a lock designed to hold fifteen barges. As they drain, it's sort of like when you were a kid and you sat in the bathtub as the bathwater drained out—except in this case, the bathtub is thirty-seven feet deep.

There is an outdoor visitor center and fishing spot that will give you a closer look without all the drama.

85

SAUERKRAUT CAVE

Why is there a cave hidden in a public park?

E.P. "Tom" Sawyer Park is a beautiful place for a picnic, a family outing, a leisurely hike, or even a swim. What many don't know is that the park was built adjacent to the former grounds of Lakeland Asylum for the Insane, which operated for most of the twentieth century, and for long stretches did so amidst controversy regarding overcrowding, questionable treatment of patients, and other malfeasances.

The cave beneath the asylum was used for storage of many things (including large cans of fermenting sauerkraut, which is how the name came about), but it was believed to have also served as a means of escape for the asylum inmates. In addition, possibly hundreds of former inmates are reported to have been buried on the property, adding to the creepiness. Meanwhile, there are rumors that the cave was also used as a place for pregnant inmates to give birth, and even reports that children of the inmates were discarded there.

In other words, the grounds around the cave are not a nice place. But it has become a destination for ghost hunters and graffiti artists, the former of which report having seen some strange things as well as having recorded ghostly voices inside the cave.

I sought out the cave alone but didn't go in. After finally tracking down the cave's location, I walked down

---

Graffiti artists seem immune to the possible haunting and have created some interesting visual tapestries around the mouth of the cave and on the cave walls.

The mouth of Sauerkraut Cave. Photo by the author.

E.P. "TOM" SAWYER PARK

WHAT A hidden cave with a mysterious back story

WHERE 3000 Freys Hill Rd.

COST Free

PRO TIP If you have trouble finding the cave, look for the archery range—you'll see a small white building adjacent to it— take the dirt road behind it down a short hill, and the path leading to the cave will be on the left.

the relatively short path to the cave, and as I approached, I felt a sudden sense of dread. Silence sets in once you are under the tree canopy, which only heightens the effect. And as I was snapping photos, I thought I heard something drop inside the cave. It was probably just water or a rock, but I couldn't get out of there quickly enough, and as I scurried away, I looked back over my shoulder two or three times to make sure nothing was following me. I'm not proud of this, but at least I'm safe.

Guided tours are offered occasionally as well. That would be my recommendation.

86

220 MILLION GALLONS OF WATER, RIGHT IN YOUR NEIGHBORHOOD

What is that fenced hilltop on Frankfort Avenue?

The Crescent Hill Reservoir and Gatehouse is another one of those places in Louisville that is used regularly and revered by those who enjoy its beauty and resources. However, many don't even know why it's there. Listed on the National Register of Historic Places, the reservoir is of great importance to Louisville and our location along the Ohio River.

Remember the quote from Samuel Taylor Coleridge's "Rime of the Ancient Mariner"? "Water, water, everywhere/ Nor any drop to drink"? That sort of described Louisville back in the 1800s when water filtration was in its infancy, and if someone handed you a glass of water, it would be brown and gritty, impure and unhealthful. Per the Louisville Water Company's website, "Old annual reports say when you got a cup of water from Louisville Water in 1860, it sometimes had some leftover mud in it."

Luckily for us, the local water company became a pioneer in researching methods of drinking water filtration, which ultimately led to the construction of what was known as the Crescent Hill Filtration Plant in the late 1800s. This undertaking was headed up in part by George Warren Fuller, who was known as "the father of sanitary engineering."

CRESCENT HILL RESERVOIR AND GATEHOUSE

WHAT A historic reservoir

WHERE Crescent Hill

COST Free

PRO TIP No swimming, but you can get some steps in and have a picnic while you're there.

The only thing more breathtaking than the giant reservoirs filled with water is the famous gatehouse. Photos by the author.

The complex encompasses a pair of elevated 110-million-gallon reservoirs, a gorgeous Gothic-style gatehouse that you can tour to this day, and a walking path around the perimeter.

The plant not only saved a lot of people from swallowing unfiltered river grit, it also became an immediate tourist attraction, with people coming from around the region by train, horse, and buggy. And it is well worth visiting today.

The perimeter of the reservoir has been converted into a walking course known as "The Mayor's Mile."

87 HAMMERHEADS

Wait, isn't that someone's basement under that shark?

Seemingly lost in the middle of the Germantown neighborhood is a little gray house at the corner of Swan and East Caldwell Streets. Well, a little gray house with a hammerhead shark mounted above the built-in garage. Yeah, that's no modest suburban home; that's Hammerheads, probably the most highly-lauded out-of-the-way place in Louisville.

> ## HAMMERHEADS
>
> **WHAT** A hole-in-the-wall eatery with a shark attached
>
> **WHERE** 921 Swan St.
>
> **COST** Varies
>
> **PRO TIP** It's the only house in the neighborhood with a hammerhead shark mounted on it.

Literally set in the basement of the one-time residence, Hammerheads isn't the first business to operate in the cramped, concrete space—my father remembers playing pinball in the place as a kid, some seventy years ago, when it was a neighborhood bar. He remembers his uncle going there to enjoy a few beers and taking my dad along. My dad was only five, so he stuck with the pinball.

Anyway, suffice to say that Hammerheads hasn't been someone's basement in a long while. And while it gets plenty of kudos around Louisville and beyond, it's amazing how many people have never dined there. Part of that may be because seating is very limited, and it's first come, first served. I was there once sitting at the bar, and the bartender told my friend and me we had to wait twenty minutes to even order food because the tiny kitchen was so far behind. But the wait was worth it.

The place looks funky, but the food is fantastic. Photos by the Author.

You'll absolutely love the food, whether it's duck fat fries, Grippo's fries, lamb ribs, a PBLT (that's a BLI made with pork belly), chicken waffles, or an elk burger.

Anyway, if you manage to get a seat at Hammerheads, you're liable to be dining either in a narrow alcove, or at a tiny counter facing out the window toward Swan Street. The restaurant opens at 4 p.m., and you'd better get there early.

It's called Hammerheads because co-owner Chase Mucerino's dad had a giant fiberglass hammerhead shark languishing in his basement. The ownership group saved it and made it a centerpiece.

88 THE VINTAGE FIRE MUSEUM

Why are there so many fire trucks in that parking lot?

Guarded by the statue of a traditional Dalmatian fire dog flanked by vintage fire trucks, the Vintage Fire Museum is an oddity in the middle of a historic downtown Jeffersonville, Indiana, an area dotted with shops and restaurants. It was conceived in 2009 and briefly opened in nearby New Albany before moving to its current location in 2012.

The space is filled with all manner of firefighting memorabilia, most of which belongs to local businessman Fred Conway. The collection was on display in his business until his untimely death in 1999, but it has since been reintroduced to the public and has also grown, thanks to a volunteer group that supports it. There are several fire trucks and other large items, but there are also models, trumpets, lanterns, and equipment, among other paraphernalia.

The museum now is used for education, events, and tours, and also features a gift shop, a space focused

---

Just a couple of blocks away is one of Jeffersonville's fire stations, across the street from which was a miniature house that firefighters used to teach fire safety to children.

VINTAGE FIRE MUSEUM

WHAT A firefighting museum

WHERE 723 Spring St. in Jeffersonville, IN

COST Free

PRO TIP The museum is on a strip of Spring St. between Court Ave. and Tenth St., and has limited hours.

This truck is one of several that can be viewed at the Vintage Fire Museum. Photos by the author.

on regional firefighting history, and an area that honors firefighters who have given their lives in the line of duty. Most of all, it is a great way to make the wide-eyed kid in your family—or inside you—squeal with delight at the colorful displays.

HOW LOUISVILLE GOT ITS NAME

Do you know who Louisville is named for?

King Louis XVI of France was sort of a pal to the early American colonies, the Commonwealth of Kentucky included. In the late 1780s, he cut a deal with Benjamin Franklin to send aid to the colonies in the form of supplies and soldiers, helping the new country gain its independence from England.

Because our founding fathers thought that was super friendly of King Louis, they decided to name a whole settlement after him which was then a part of the Commonwealth of Virginia—it later became part of the Commonwealth of Kentucky when the latter was ratified as a state.

Today, Louisville is a sister city to Montpelier, France, and a nearly-two-hundred-year-old statue of King Louis XVI, created by French sculptor Achille-Joseph Valois and gifted to the city in 1967, now stands twelve feet tall downtown at Louisville Metro Hall.

The next time you hear someone call the city "Lou-uh-vul," you can point out to them that there was never a King Lou-uh XVI of France.

King Louis XVI stands guard at Louisville Metro Hall. Photo by Bedford/Wikimedia Commons.

LOUISVILLE, KY

WHAT The city's namesake

WHERE Here

COST Free

PRO TIP Practice saying it if it helps: Loo-ee-ville. Loo-ee-ville.

INDEX